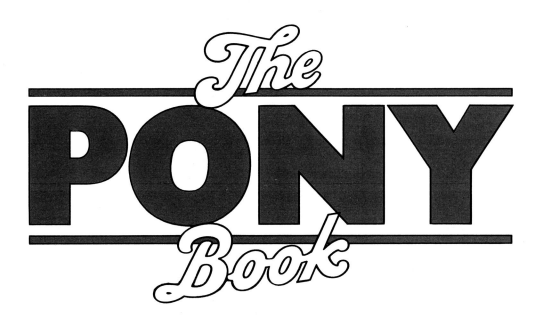

compiled by Nancy Roberts

Editor of PONY

Foreword by Lesley McNaught

Christmas 1985
Love E.M.M.A xx

COLLINS

William Collins Sons & Co. Ltd
London · Glasgow · Sydney · Auckland
Toronto · Johannesburg

ISBN 0 00 195389 3
First published 1984
© William Collins Sons & Co. Ltd 1984
Photoset by Rowland Phototypesetting Ltd
Bury St Edmunds, Suffolk
Printed in Italy

Line drawings by Sally Bell, Jane Ettridge, Ian McIntosh
Photographs specially taken by Kit Houghton

designed by Linda Sullivan

Contents

HANDS OFF!

THIS BOOK BELONGS TO

Bianca Lignell.

Lesley McNaught says...

"I suppose I've been horse mad all my life — although it wasn't until I was about ten or eleven and I started competing that I began to dream of being a top show jumper. Like most ambitions it has taken a lot of hard work, and a fair helping of luck, to succeed but it has been worth every minute.

"This book should set any young rider on the right path. I only wish I'd had something like it when I had my ponies. It wasn't until I joined Ted and Liz Edgar's yard at the advanced age of sixteen that I discovered that I didn't really know a thing about horses. I thought all you had to do was sit on top and jump a clear round! They taught me the intricacies of schooling and the real art of riding.

"Not that riding is all hard work, far from it! As you'll discover from this book, there's a vast amount of fun to be had with horses and the opportunity to build up a wonderful partnership with your favourites. Although I've been lucky enough to ride a great many good horses there are some that will always hold a special place in my heart.

"I hope you too will have as much fun from riding as I have — and I'm sure *The Pony Book* will help you enjoy every minute.**"**

Enjoying Ponies

The ultimate ambition for most pony enthusiasts is actually to own a pony! Unfortunately many have to make do with riding other people's ponies. It's not quite the same but it's not the end of the world. The people who get the most fun out of ponies are not necessarily the ones that have their own. They are the people who realise that there's more to ponies than riding and that you can have a lot of fun just watching them, looking after them and getting to know them.

Riding Schools

If you don't have your own pony you may find that you are able to get rides with horsy friends but if you have never ridden before I think the best thing to do is to find a really good riding school and go as often as you can afford to, within reason. The advantages of paying to ride are that you are not constantly relying on someone else's generosity. Provided you book, there will always be a pony available for you and as you will be riding with other people who don't have their own ponies, you won't feel left out! A good school will have a friendly atmosphere and, most important, give you correct instruction in riding and pony care which will be essential if (when) you get a pony of your own.

Riding schools have to be licensed by your local council, but unfortunately this is not a very reliable guide as to whether the school is a really good one or not. To find out where the best schools are in your area write (enclosing a stamped, addressed envelope) to the British Horse Society, British Equestrian Centre, Stoneleigh, Kenilworth, Warwickshire, CV8 2LR. They run an approval scheme and their inspectors keep a sharp eye on teaching standards, welfare of ponies and facilities offered to clients.

When you have found a few addresses, ring up and ask to look round. The yard should be reasonably tidy, the ponies well fed and clean (unless they are in a field when they can be forgiven for being covered in mud) and there should be a friendly atmosphere about the place. Riders should all be wearing hard hats – this is essential. Many schools lend hats to new clients, but you will be expected to buy your own eventually. If you don't have riding boots, strong, preferably lace-up shoes are also needed, not wellingtons or gym shoes. You don't need to buy jodhpurs at first, as jeans or other well-fitting trousers will do; in time though, you'll find they can slide up your legs and chafe.

Most schools take rides out around the district, called "hacking", but they should also have a decent field or outdoor manège (a prepared riding surface) where beginners can be taught. Many have indoor schools, cross country courses and show jumps for more ambitious pupils.

Many centres organize their own shows and competitions, and lectures or demonstrations on pony care. They may run clubs or "Own a Pony" days in the school holidays, when clients can look after one of the school ponies for a day, riding, grooming, feeding and generally being responsible for it.

You don't need your own pony to enjoy a ride in the country.

It is very important to have *good* lessons when you are learning to ride because a pony which frightens you or a poor instructor can put you off for life. If you are taught incorrectly, even if you are enjoying yourself at the time, you will find it is twice as hard to unlearn your bad habits later. So do be careful about picking a good school which you like.

Pony Club

If you have your own pony, you can join your local branch of The Pony Club (headquarters at the British Equestrian Centre). As a member, you will be taught riding and pony care at regular rallies and get the chance to compete in mounted games, dressage, jumping and maybe even inter-branch events.

The Pony Club is particularly valuable for pony owners who perhaps can't afford regular lessons. There will always be someone experienced around to give advice if it's needed and most branches hold a summer camp where members can take their ponies for a week's instruction. They also have quite a lot of social events, especially in the winter when the weather may be too poor for mounted rallies. Quizzes, film shows and discos are a good opportunity to meet new horsy friends and for your branch to do some fund raising for the summer's activities.

Shows

Aside from Pony Club events, there are countless shows and gymkhanas which are fun for spectators and riders. Gymkhanas are mounted games – potato races, sack races or bending races amongst others; lots of fun and not requiring particular talent, at least at local levels.

At smaller shows you'll also see classes for Fancy Dress, Best Turned Out and Handy Pony where competitors have to negotiate a course of hazards like a row of plastic sacks, a gate to open, a trailer to walk through and other tests of their pony's obedience.

Larger shows will also have showing and jumping classes, Best Rider competitions and possibly in-hand breed and youngstock classes.

Showing classes are judged on a pony's conformation, action and manners. Both pony and rider must be immaculately turned out with the pony schooled to go smoothly wherever the rider wishes, change from one pace to another without argument, and not misbehave by bucking, pulling, kicking or biting the judge! (It does happen!) By watching these classes carefully you'll find you can develop your eye for a good pony and try your hand at "ringside judging".

Jumping classes always draw the biggest crowds and nowadays there is a great deal of money involved in it, even at junior levels. If you think you'd like to try showjumping, it is best to start with a fun beginners' class to get the feel of riding in the ring, gradually progressing through novice and open grades as you become more experienced.

If you get hooked on showing or jumping you will discover it is a very competitive world. Quality ponies can be hard to find, are very expensive, and at the top, the pressure on all concerned is severe. At national level, riders compete on a regular circuit of major county shows, and you will find your life almost completely taken up with it all. As well as needing financial backing you must be single-minded and truly dedicated, as standards are extremely high if you are to win anything worthwhile.

Horse Trials

Unlike show jumping with its coloured, artificial fences, cross-country competitions or hunter trials are a test of the horse's ability to get its rider safely across the countryside. The jumps met are natural hazards such as ditches, fences and gates often fixed and, in top class events, an imposing test of both rider's and horse's skill and courage. Again, it is best to start small at local competitions, where you can enjoy an exhilarating ride across country.

Showjumping and cross-country are two of the three tests which make up a Horse Trials or One Day Event. The third phase is dressage, the French word for "training", which is a test of the horse's basic schooling. Competitors ride a series of movements which they have learnt by heart, rather like a dance routine. It really isn't difficult and your riding instructor or Pony Club will be able to teach you more about it.

At a One Day Event riders will probably do a dressage test in the morning followed by the showjumping phase, with cross-country in the afternoon. At major international competitions such as Badminton or Burghley these phases are spread over three or four days, hence the name Three Day Eventing. They are becoming increasingly popular to watch and make a great day out in the country.

A smart turn-out is essential if you are entering a showing class.

A working hunter pony class combines showing with jumping.

Hacking

Although today's world seems to be competition mad, it is not everyone's idea of fun. If you don't really like competing there are still plenty of other horse activities to choose from.

One of these is hacking. Unfortunately, as our countryside becomes more built up and roads busier, safe places to ride are more and more scarce. So before you venture out, make sure your pony is traffic proof and not liable to shy at a frightening object or vehicle.

It is great fun getting to know an area from the back of a pony. The view from the saddle is quite different from the one you get low down in a car or perched on a bike. You can see over hedges and enjoy views you never noticed before.

If you get an Ordnance Survey map from your local stationer you can find and follow the bridlepaths in your district. These paths are rights of way so if one is blocked, report it to the local Bridleways Officer of the British Horse Society. You will be providing a valuable public service by helping keep them open, and you could further this work by joining your local bridleways group.

Hacking is one way to get really close to a pony. They enjoy going out far more than being ridden in the same field or indoor school all the time. And when the pony is enjoying himself, you'll enjoy yourself all the more.

Below Hacking is a great way to enjoy the countryside, but do remember to close gates behind you. *Right* A welcome break for competitors during the Golden Horseshoe long distance ride on Exmoor.

Long Distance Riding

Long distance riding is one sport where you compete only against yourself. Sounds strange? It isn't really. You simply have to cover a given number of miles within a certain length of time, keeping your pony well and happy. In its simplest form, long distance riding is called "Competitive Trail Riding", and at the other end of the scale, "Endurance Riding", which demands quite a lot of skill and preparation. At the advanced stage, some of these events do take the form of a race, the first one home *in good condition* being the winner.

Start long distance riding by entering local "sponsored rides" which will vary between 5 and 25 miles. They give you the opportunity to ride through the countryside in the company of others and will help you develop a feel of pace and distance. If you'd like to progress you could join the Endurance Horse and Pony Society based at 6 Lundy View, Northam, Bideford, Devon. The British Horse Society also have a Long Distance Riding Group.

Hunting

There are four types of hunting for riders – foxhunting, hare or stag-hunting and drag hunting. In the latter, hounds follow a ready-laid trail and do not chase a living animal. Drag hunting is fast and courses are often laid out over quite difficult jumps, so you usually find the standard of riding is higher than in some other hunts.

The kind of ride you will get is largely determined by the countryside in which you hunt. In grass country you will probably have a lot of galloping and jumping, on moors there will be hazards such as rivers, bogs and steep slopes to contend with, and in more enclosed or "trappy" areas, the pace will be slower and the jumps more awkward.

Hunting has a set of manners and behaviour all its own, and the arguments for and against the hunting and killing of live animals with a pack of hounds are many and varied. You will doubtless make up your own mind about this and be guided by your own conscience, but, from a riding point of view only, it can be an enjoyable day out and excellent education for both pony and rider.

Foxhounds

HANDY HINT

Ponies enjoy a gallop but some can get a bit over excited! If you are afraid you can't stop, steer the pony into a circle, gradually making it smaller until he slows down. If this doesn't work, shorten your reins and pull on them alternately and quite sharply, sitting well down into the saddle. Leaning forward will encourage him to go faster.

Out of the Saddle

What about those long winter evenings when it is too dark to ride and ponies are all tucked up in bed asleep? Plenty of people still follow their hobby without actually riding at all.

How about finding out as much as you can about one particular breed of horse or pony, collecting pictures and articles about it from magazines such as PONY, and making a scrapbook. You can take books out of your local library for more information or take your own snapshots at shows where that breed appears. Ask the owners about the animal you photograph so that you can put details with the photo in your book – the animal's name, breeding, sex, height and age, and its major wins.

This form of project can be followed in a similar way for almost any aspect of the horse world. You could follow the career of your favourite showjumper or eventer, using a loose leaf book to paste up news-clippings, articles from magazines and autographs like a biography.

You could also make a project like this about your own or favourite riding school pony. Over several years, this will build up into a unique record you will treasure and enjoy re-reading.

Of course, some projects have a practical value too. Why not start your own Activity Record for your pony, detailing the shows and events you go to, how he does or what he wins? "Jumped well out hunting" or "Won Novice Jumping class", for instance. Keep a note of his health at the same time as it can be helpful for your vet to know his pattern of feed, management and exercise, should your pony become ill.

You can develop your own Master Diary, noting important dates such as shows you are attending, when vaccinations are due, farriers' appointments and your own holidays.

Finally, you could start a collection of model horses and ponies; there are many different makes and even clubs for model owners. And a library of good pony books is a valuable education in itself.

Horses and ponies will give you enjoyment all your life. Why not start right now?

Choosing a Pony

Type and temperament are the two magic words when choosing a pony. Choosing the right type is a practical matter; obviously you will want a pony which is the right size and which you can manage easily, and it will also have to thrive in the facilities you have to offer.

Temperament

Temperament is a rather more emotional subject. Choosing a pony is like choosing a friend. If opposing temperaments rub, you can't even begin to build a relationship. If, for example, you lose your temper easily and choose a sensitive pony, you will break its heart; whereas if you are ambitious and choose a slug, it will break yours. The answer to this is to take a hard, honest look at yourself, at your own temperament and ambitions, and then to choose a pony with whom you can form a partnership.

Type

Whether you are looking for a pony to buy or borrow, the type you choose will depend on the facilities available. If these are limited to a paddock or shared grazing, then a native pony, be it pure-bred or cross-bred, will suit you very well. A native will generally thrive on a diet of grass supplemented with hay as necessary, and in the winter will grow an enormously thick coat as protection from the cold and wet. As long as it is "well covered" (the outline of native ponies should be rounded rather than angular, and you shouldn't be able to see their ribs), it will be perfectly happy, and though it may give you a pang to see your pony with a crust of snow on its rump, remember that natives are designed to live outside all the year round!

A happy partnership

Choosing a Pony

The main distinctions between the native breeds are in size and build. Thus the tiny, powerful Shetland is mainly suited to driven activities and as a leading-rein mount and family pet, although determined little riders often manage them very well. For the same reason, the larger, heavily built Highland, Fell and Dales ponies are eminently suitable for trekking and for carrying adult and heavyweight riders, although they are hardly ever seen in the gymkhana rings.

Of the larger native ponies, the Connemara and New Forest breeds have proved themselves the most popular mounts for young people, and of the smaller varieties, the Dartmoor, Exmoor, and more especially the Welsh have consistently shown their worth. The joy of the natives is that at their best, they are hardy, resistant to disease, economical and labour-saving, strong, sensible and friendly. Obviously you will pay more for a purebred native showing the distinct characteristics of the breed and having papers to prove it, but many worthy ponies are crossbred, their ancestry somewhat obscure, and none the worse for that.

If your facilities include a stable as well as grazing, additional help and sufficient funds for rugs and corn feeds, then you could choose a riding pony. The modern riding pony is a carefully developed hybrid, usually the result of crossing a Thoroughbred with a native pony, then crossing the result back to another native. The end product of this is a small Thoroughbred with definite pony characteristics. It is beautiful, fast, courageous, thin-coated and elegant; wonderful for showing and competition work, but also requiring plenty of attention. It wasn't bred to live outdoors all year round and it would be heartless to expect it to – also, being a bit high-powered, it needs an experienced rider and is not a pony for the novice or faint-hearted. Again, you will probably pay more for a riding pony registered with the National Pony Society, but there are others who are not, and with a bit of practice you will be able to spot whether a pony is predominantly a native or riding pony type.

Suitability
When choosing a pony, it is important not to overmount yourself. If you are a novice rider, a novice pony will not suit you at all; what you need is an older, experienced "schoolmaster", too set in his ways to learn new mischief, and the sort you need to push on, rather than hold back. This will help you develop a confident, effective seat so that afterwards you will be ready to tackle a livelier or younger mount. If you are already experienced and have ambitions towards something specific, like jumping or eventing, you should have a clear idea of your own ability and requirements anyway, but take care – you must be capable of keeping the upper hand!

Size
We have mentioned temperament, type and suitability; now on to the knotty problem of size. If you intend to compete, you are obviously governed by classification and this will dictate the height of pony you choose; apart from this, you may feel that the world is your oyster and you can choose a pony as small or as big as you wish. Not so. If you ride a pony too big or too small you will feel insecure, your balance will be impaired, your aids won't be received in the right places, and control will be more difficult. Trying ponies of assorted sizes is the best way to prove that when you are mounted on a pony of the right size you feel right, you look right and your performance benefits accordingly.

Above left
Overhorsed. *Above*
right **Underhorsed!**

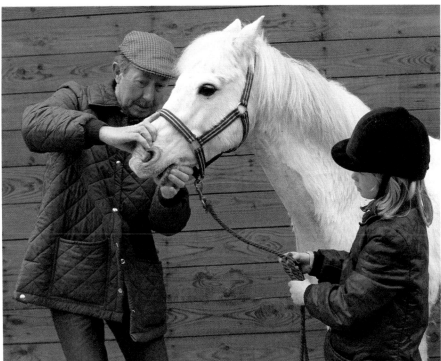

Right **Any potential
buy should be vetted
before you finally
decide.**

Health

Soundness is a matter for your veterinary surgeon. Do not consider buying a pony without having it vetted first. Your vet will, on the strength of his examination, advise you whether or not you should go ahead with the purchase. Having paid well for his advice, take it!

19

The Points of a pony

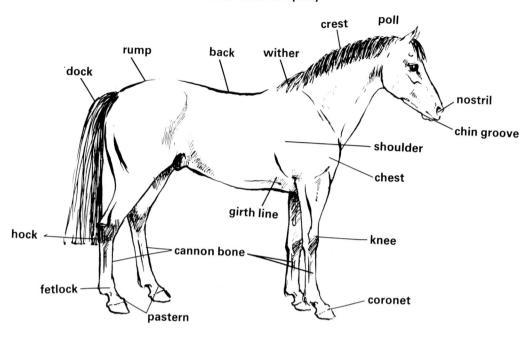

Pony with good conformation

Conformation

Conformation is another matter. If a pony is correctly built, it will move easily and lightly with its head carried naturally in the right place. If, for example, you ride a pony with a short, thick neck set upon a straight shoulder you will find it almost impossible to achieve balance and collection; all that will happen is that you have a heavy weight in your hands. Likewise, if you ride a pony who has an unnaturally high headcarriage, because its neck is set on "upside down" (with the muscle bulk *under* the neck instead of on top) it will throw it even higher when you try to collect it, and martingales will only result in a hollow back, impaired action, and an irritated, uncomfortable pony. The sad thing is that it isn't the pony's fault, and while masses of patient schooling might improve matters, it can't work miracles – you wouldn't expect to make an Olympic athlete out of someone who was knock-kneed and splay footed, after all!

From this, you will see that correct conformation is important and the only way to develop an eye for a well-made pony is to look critically at every one you see – in the flesh and in photographs.

The ideal pony should have a small, intelligent-looking head, with a large, kind eye, and small, sharp ears. It should have an elegant-looking long neck, set onto a sloping, rather than upright shoulder, ending in a well-defined wither. Its back should be compact rather than long, its rump rounded rather than angular, and its tail should be set so that in movement it is carried gaily and naturally, neither clamped down angrily to the pony's rump, nor waving above like a banner.

When viewed from the side, the ideal pony should be deep through the chest (girth line), and it should stand naturally four-square and straight, so that the line from the hock to the fetlock is vertical. Long, spindly cannon bones are a sign of weakness, as are long, straight pasterns. From the front, the chest should be wide enough for there to be another foreleg in the middle, and the feet should be regular-shaped and open – not tall and boxy like a donkey's.

Movement

Conformation is an exhaustive subject and the more you learn about it, the more you realize that, as in the human race, equine perfection is rare, and most of us have to be content with rather less – in which case correct movement is as important, if not more important, as correct conformation. To assess movement ask someone to trot the pony up and down for you.

A trotting pony, viewed from the front, should move towards you in a straight line – any legs which swing out of true, inwards or outwards, are a weakness, and any pony which actually knocks itself is obviously a disaster! The pony should cover the ground easily with long, flowing stride, and its head carried naturally in the right place. Such a pony is naturally balanced and, even if not perfect conformation-wise, is a much better buy than one who lumbers along with lowered head and trailing hocks, scraping the ground with its hooves – unfortunately, a common sight.

Temperament

Manners may be made when the pony is broken and schooled, but even the best pony in the world can be spoiled if indulged by a weak or nervous rider. A strong-minded pony needs an equally strong-minded rider, and spiteful animals should

A good pony should be a comfortable ride. One which goes on the forehand *left* will be tiring for its rider, while a pony which is above the bit *right* will be difficult to control.

be avoided at all costs: a lighthearted buck is one thing, but a pony who really tries to throw you off is quite another. Keep well away from rearers and think long and hard before buying a highly-strung pony who shies a lot, however good a rider you may be. These days no one can afford to take chances in traffic and a pony who is continually looking for things to spook at is a menace. Likewise, if you can't stop the pony you are riding, whether it is because your seat isn't strong enough, or because he has a mouth like iron, don't choose it!

Ponies are like people; they vary enormously in temperament and character. Some simply adore human company, will happily submit to being groomed all day long, and will whicker in pleasure when they see you approach. Others loathe being fussed over, are irritated by grooming, turn their backs on you, and nip you when they get the chance. You don't need me to tell you which kind are easier to love.

Temperament is carried over into performance as well; if a pony enjoys being ridden and does what you ask of it willingly, riding is a joy; but if the pony is a misery, if it won't try for you, then it can be a depressing business.

Remember two magic words, type and temperament; to which you must add size, suitability, conformation and movement – and good luck in your search for the perfect pony.

> **HANDY HINT**
> If your pony is nervous of traffic try turning him out in a field near a main road so that he can get used to the noise gradually. On rides an older reliable pony between him and the traffic will also help to build up his confidence.
>
> ● ● ●
>
> Most ponies don't buck maliciously, they do it for fun, but it can still be very unseating! If your pony starts to buck, shorten your reins quickly, pull his head up and ride him on.

Below left Beware of buying ponies at an auction, however appealing. They could be unsound, unbroken and unstable.
Below right Never buy a rearer. It's a difficult vice to break and if the pony overbalanced you could be badly hurt.

Pony Breeds

Altogether there are nine different native pony breeds in Britain. The stocky Dales and Fell from the North were once used as pack ponies. Dartmoor and Exmoor ponies have roamed the moorland of Devon and Somerset since medieval times. Hampshire is the home of the New Forest pony while Wales has no less than four different types, ranging from the pretty Welsh Mountain to the sturdy cob. The Shetland and Highland come from Scotland and the Connemara from Ireland.

A hundred years ago they were an essential means of transport in country areas and would often be used to work the farmland as well. Nowadays they make hardy and versatile riding ponies for both children and adults.

Below New Forest stallion. *Over the page* Highland stallion and mares. Strong and hardy they make ideal trekking ponies.

Above Exmoors are one of the most ancient British breeds. They have characteristic "mealy" muzzles and eyes and should not be bigger than 12·3hh.

Left Unlike other breeds the Shetland is measured in inches not hands. Their average height is 38″ but they are extremely strong and quite capable of carrying an adult!

Right The Welsh Mountain is one of the prettiest native ponies and is often seen in the show ring especially in leading rein classes. Measuring up to 12hh they are quite narrow and so are popular rides for small children.

Where Will He Live?

In an ideal world every pony would have access to a field and a stable. He could graze and stretch his legs in his field, but have the comfort of a stable in the really bad, or really hot weather.

However, this is not an ideal world, and many ponies have to put up with either a field, or a stable. Most ponies can adjust to whatever lifestyle is offered, but at either end of the scale you have exceptions. Small, busy, native ponies are not going to enjoy an exclusively indoor life, and a finely bred, thin skinned riding pony will not winter out happily, however many rugs you pile upon him.

If your pony is going to have to spend a lot of time in a stable he will need to be comfortable. A pony of up to 13.2hh will be fine in a 10′ × 10′ box but a larger pony will be happier in a 12′ × 12′ loose box. The box should have a divided door, to allow free circulation of air and so that the pony can look out. The top door should only really be closed if the pony is very ill or rain and snow are driving directly into the stable. Bear in mind when siting the doorway that a pony is a gregarious creature and likes to see what is going on, and also that the doorway needs a certain protection from the prevailing wind. A window will let in light and help ventilation and should preferably be hopper style, opening inwards but protected by bars to prevent the pony breaking the glass with its nose.

If a pony is going to live inside most of the time then a concrete floor is necessary as it is easier to keep clean and dry than earth or chalk. The stable floor should slope slightly to a drain, but it is possible to manage without. It is important to remember that the floor must be non-slip so the concrete should have a rough surface. It is very helpful if the concrete standing outside the stable slopes away slightly to prevent water from running into the stable.

Prefabricated wooden loose boxes are excellent and there are plenty of makes to choose from; the more expensive ones will include internal kicking boards and metal edging to doors and fittings to prevent nibbling. Both these are worth the extra cost.

Concrete or brick stables are possibly less warm than wooden stables, but are more robust. Extra bedding banked up against concrete walls should solve the problem of heat loss.

Ideally a stable should be fitted with a manger, a hayrack, a salt lick holder, and a ring for tying. However, a moveable plastic manger which attaches to the door or a bucket or bowl on the floor is quite satisfactory for feeding and haynets are often better than racks for very small ponies. It is important to have a suitable ring for fixing the haynet, as ponies can get their feet caught in a net if it is too low or becomes untied. Self-filling waterbowls are a labour saving way of supplying a stable with water but are really only worth the expense in a big yard. One or two large rubber buckets are quite sufficient as long as they are cleaned and re-filled at least two or three times a day.

Years ago a horse was reckoned to need at least an acre of land. Now many pony paddocks are less than one third of an acre. The smaller the field, the better the fencing must be as the pony is more likely to get bored, stick his head through the wire, lean on weak places or chew wooden bars. Post and rail fencing is ideal but expensive; plain wire is preferable to barbed wire but it must be kept taut and carefully fixed to stout posts. Fences must be secure *before* the pony is turned out. A pony who gets a taste for escaping will become more and more difficult to confine and a habitual escaper is a menace. Loopy, slack wire, wobbling, half-rotten posts, bundles of barbed wire and bedsteads are positively dangerous. If the field is partly fenced in that manner then re-fence that bit.

The pony must have a constant supply of fresh water, be it a trough, a bath or regularly filled buckets. Buckets are the least satisfactory method as a pony who knocks over his water bucket might then have to wait 24 hours for another drink.

Post and rails make secure fencing. A net stops hay from being wasted in the field, while racks are often fitted in stables.

29

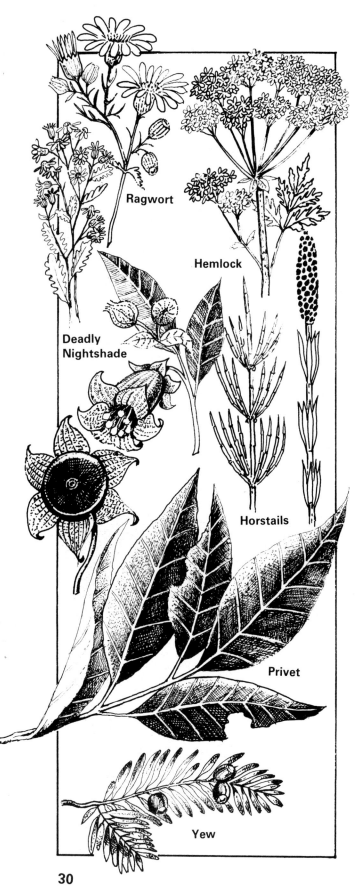

Ragwort

Hemlock

Deadly
Nightshade

Horstails

Privet

Yew

Here are some of the more common poisonous plants which you should watch out for in fields and hedgerows.

Ragwort A yellow-flowered common weed of the dandelion family which spreads rapidly and should be uprooted immediately it starts to appear in your field. Its presence usually indicates that the grass is in poor condition.

Hemlock This highly poisonous plant has a purple spotted stem and white flowers which resemble Cow Parsley. It is found in dampish places by roads and streams.

Deadly Nightshade This plant even looks deadly! It has dull, greeny/purple flowers and extremely poisonous black, cherry-sized berries. It is found in shady places on chalk or limestone.

Horsetails These green plants are smaller descendants of the giant horsetails of the dinosaur age. They are very difficult to dig up as their roots go down a long way. But any of them in your field should be got rid of immediately.

Privet You are unlikely to find wild privet in the hedges surrounding your field, but do watch out for garden privet. Don't chat to a friend while your pony idly chews a privet hedge!

Yew Yew is often propagated by birds dropping the seeds and very small yew trees may be found in the most unlikely places. Keep a careful watch as they are deadly. Watch out too for any fallen branches from a large yew tree that may have landed in your pony's field. Clear them away immediately. Yew is as dangerous as Deadly Nightshade.

If your pony is well-bred or you want him to do much work in the winter then he will need to be clipped out, rugged up and stabled at night. This means that you will be committed to visiting him at least twice a day and exercising him whatever the weather. However if your pony has some native blood then he should be able to cope with winter winds and rain and may be turned out for longer periods although he may still require a New Zealand rug and a field shelter. A shelter is useful as you can leave your pony's hay and food away from the rain, you can use it as a temporary stable, say before a show, and you do not have to worry too much about your pony in the really bad weather. With a paddock and a field shelter, you could cope with a fairly finely-bred pony, checking and changing New Zealand rugs twice a day, and making sure he has sufficient hay and food.

If you do not have facilities to keep a pony at home, then you will have to keep him at livery. Livery is another word for "lodging". For around £5 a week you should be able to "park" your pony in a field but this is unlikely to include any extra feed or facilities. In the winter your pony will need hay and probably hard feed and this is often arranged either with the field owner or with the owners of the other ponies.

If your pony is to live out all year round he will need to be tough and not nervous of others or he will lose out at dinner time and will probably not do well. Some field owners will agree to check the ponies and water each day, and maybe feed them, but you cannot expect someone else to check and change rugs. This type of grass livery is best suited to a less racy, more substantial and woolly pony; clipping is certainly not recommended.

A "do-it-yourself" livery yard usually offers the use of a stable, a small paddock and sometimes facilities such as an indoor

Above A pony that lives out all the year round needs shelter from wind and rain. *Below* Extra padding at the shoulders will stop a New Zealand rug from rubbing.

Ponies are gregarious creatures and like company when they're turned out.

school or jumps. The snag is that you have to do all the work. You must visit your pony twice a day, to feed, muck out, turn out, bring in, bed and feed – that is to say nothing of riding. This is difficult to combine with school and homework, especially in the winter. Some yards have a rota system to share work but you must decide first if you really could cope with, say, six ponies before and after school, even if it is only for one day of the week. If you're planning to turn your pony out in a New Zealand rug so that he can exercise himself, find out first if the yard has facilities for drying the rug,

otherwise you might find yourself dragging it home on a bicycle!

Full livery, when someone else looks after your pony completely, including exercising, is marvellous but expensive.

During the summer, life is much easier. If you plan to do a lot of competition work, then a stable is necessary as it is very difficult to produce a really fit, well turned out pony if he lives out all the time. If your pony gets very fat, or suffers from laminitis, he will need to be stabled and kept on a diet. A pony prone to sweet itch is also best kept inside during summer days.

Pony Type	Facilities	Feed and Equipment	Owner's Daily Worksheet
clipped pony	stable only	hay, concentrates, night rug	½ hour minimum morning and evening for rug changing, mucking out plus exercise time
	stable and paddock	as above, plus New Zealand rug	as above. Exercise time not essential as pony turned out for part of day
	full livery	as above	pony will be cared for and exercised by groom. Owner rides when wishes
unclipped finely bred pony	stable and paddock	hay, concentrates, New Zealand rug, night rug	½ hour morning and evening for feeding, mucking out rug changing, turning out
	field	as above but 2 New Zealand rugs	½ hour morning and evening for feeding, changing rugs (to allow one to dry)
large native pony	stable and paddock	hay and concentrates	½ hour morning, mucking out, turning out, ¼ hour evening for catching up and feeding
	field	hay and concentrates in winter	10 minutes daily to check over and feed in winter
small native pony	field	hay in bad weather or if grass is poor	as above

HANDY HINT

If your pony is turned out during the day but stabled at night, muck out in the morning and bank the clean bedding around the walls of the box. This will give the stable a chance to air and the floor to dry out.

Famous People's Ponies

Do you ever wonder how your favourite showjumper or eventer made it to the top? It may be hard to imagine but, just like you, they probably started off on a little 12.2hh, falling off in the bending race or being eliminated in the Beginners Jumping! Here a few of our top riders describe their first steps.

David Broome, who insists that he cannot possibly remember how long he has been a showjumper (adding at the same time that riding for a living beats working for it), is possibly Britain's best-loved rider. There's hardly a single major event which he hasn't won, from world championships to Olympic medals and Grand Prix classes all over the world. But David had to start somewhere too.

"To tell you the truth I can't remember my first pony. My family always had ponies, and I'm told I began riding properly when I was three. But I don't recall what on . . .

"My first good pony, was a little 13.2hh chestnut mare called Coffee, and she wasn't at all bad! Some people don't like chestnut mares as they say they have a funny temperament, but Coffee certainly didn't. She was just fine.

"I suppose I must have been about eight or nine years old at the time and we did masses of different classes together; hunter trials, gymkhanas, showjumping, all sorts.

"The only thing which was a little awkward was the steep way she always landed from a jump. Not that I really knew any different as I'd not jumped many ponies then. But Coffee landed almost vertically sometimes, which was a bit unnerving!

"Coffee was followed by two other ponies, both geldings, when I was about ten. One was called Chocolate and the other was my famous pony Ballan Lad. Lad was Welsh and lived until he was 37 years old – though I'm obliged to say that that's not a record for age. I've heard of ponies living to be over 40!"

It was a dreadfully sad moment for the Broome family when Ballan Lad died in 1982. "He had colic, and a minor heart failure and the vet said the old boy only had 36 hours to live. So we had him put down painlessly and peacefully; it was very sad. We'd all had fun with him, and learned so much."

Lucinda Green is probably the idol of every horse-mad girl. From the moment in April 1973 when she first won Badminton Horse Trials (she's won it another five times since) Lucinda has been Britain's top lady event rider. But where did this talented young lady make her start?

"The pony which I first rode with any degree of seriousness was a pretty little grey 14.2hh mare which we had bought and named Sea Sway. I owe her a lot; it was only because I had outgrown her that Mummy and I decided that it was time to go and find something bigger. I would have needed roller skates if I'd wanted to carry on riding Sea Sway. My legs were getting so long, I almost touched the ground.

"Because of that we followed up an advertisement in Horse and Hound for the sole progeny of a recent Burghley Three Day Event winner named Fair and Square. Be Fair was my first proper horse, nearly 16.2hh and over eight inches bigger than little Sea Sway!

"One feature both had in common, especially in the early days, was a marked reluctance to enter a trailer! Sea Sway needed most emphatic encouragement and lengthy persuasion – and so did Be Fair, at first. In due course they both were taught that it is easier to go in first time.

"My transition from ponies to horses was consequently rather sudden! 15.2hh is the generally recognised 'stepping stone' height between ponies and horses, and I had always imagined that when the time came for Sea Sway to be sold, that was what I would buy. Not so. I was 14 years old and growing fast so a 16.2hh seemed natural.

"I also wanted a new saddle as I'd learned to ride in a pre-war polo saddle! To win a new one, I had to enter a St John's Ambulance 30-mile sponsored ride on the Downs near Newbury, in Berkshire. The final realization that Sea Sway was not up to this, but that Be Fair might be, was really the end of my partnership with the little mare. Be Fair won the saddle! Sea Sway was sold to a very nice family in Norfolk.

"I remember riding Be Fair while my friend Lucilla rode Sea Sway in the pairs class at a local Pony Club Hunter Trials. It was remarkable for two reasons. Be Fair finally learned to stop whipping round to the right and rearing in front of fences and we won the pairs. The two of them went brilliantly despite their difference in height. It was the only red rosette Be Fair and I won for two years!"

Opposite David Broome on Mr Ross. *Below* Lucinda Green on Regal Realm tackling a water jump

Pat Smythe is probably the most famous lady showjumper of all. She was the first woman to be allowed to compete in an Olympic showjumping event, and is still one of very few riders to have jumped a clear round in the Derby at Hickstead.

But it wasn't always like that for Pat. Her first pony was a small hairy grey named Bubbles, which she rode around her local Richmond Park, toes firmly at right-angles to the stirrup leathers. It was not until her mother, Monica, realized that ballet lessons were the cause, that Pat's somewhat unorthodox foot position was cured!

"Pixie was the pony of my dreams. She was a handsome chestnut of about 13hh, five years old and very spirited with a will of her own. Her mother was a Dartmoor, her father an Arab and she was bred on the Royal Farm at Tor Royal, no less. From the moment we saw her, I wanted her for my own and there seemed little more that life could offer when my parents announced that we would buy her at once and take her home to Richmond.

"I took some hard knocks and falls, and no pony ever bucked me off as much as Pixie! Her rodeo displays often attracted an audience yet we established a deep relationship. She had a phenomenal spring and, though she was cautious, she always jumped big. So big that I frequently fell off! She was brilliant at gymkhanas, and turned into a very good pony. We won our first big event at Richmond Horse Show in 1939. She eventually lost the sight of one eye after being kicked but jumped even better afterwards! She would always take red walls from a complete standstill – after giving them a good look first!"

Michael Whitaker and his brother John are both leading international show-jumpers. Michael is now most famous for his breathtaking sprint finishes with horses like Overton Amanda and Disney Way, but, just like you and me, he started small!

"My first pony was a very good 12.2hh liver chestnut gelding called Merrydale Penrose. He was a real schoolmaster whom we bought locally, from a family which had done a lot of showing with him. He proved to have a liking for jumping and began winning for me right from the word 'go'! He took to jumping like a duck takes to water.

"Basically he enjoyed the sport, and still does. I only rode him for about three summers, and then I went onto a 14.2hh. Merrydale must be well into his teens now but he's still jumping like a stag.

"His only fault was his stable manners. He was fine out at grass, and at shows . . . but he kicked and bit in his stable, and used to become very irritable if he was kept shut in for long spells. In the ring though, he was terrific and never put a foot wrong. He could win 13.2hh classes and surprised us all one day by clearing a 5′2″ fence – I was about twelve at the time.

My next memorable pony was Tamarisk, a really good 14.2hh, which I rode when I was about fifteen or sixteen. I didn't do a lot with him because he tended to put in a stop occasionally. But he was good on his day, and then he could beat them all. He and I won the Leading Junior Show Jumper award at the Horse of the Year Show. Then I went on to horses . . ."

Opposite Pat Smythe on Scorching. *Below* Michael Whitaker competing at Wembley

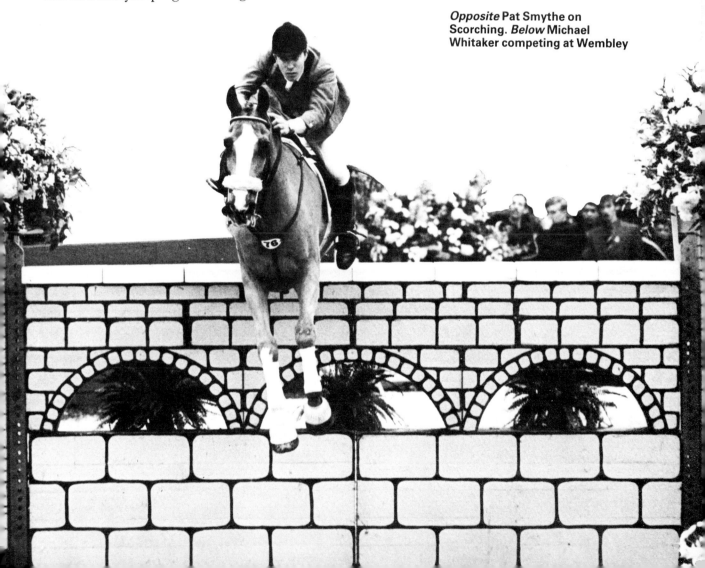

Lesley McNaught, hailed by many as "a new Pat Smythe", was given the chance of a lifetime to enter serious show jumping. She was jumping a 12.2hh pony called Skipalong at a local show near her home town of Hinckley when she was spotted by Liz Edgar. She left school on her 16th birthday in February 1980, joined the Edgar's yard and has never once looked back.

"My very, very first pony was called Curi, which was short for Curiosity. He was very old when I began riding him but he taught me an awful lot. My mother used to ride him in his younger days, and so did my sister.

"Then I progressed to Little Cracker, who was just that – a terrific little dun gymkhana pony. Fantastic fun! But my absolute favourite was a 13.2hh named Golden Arrow VI, and he became my 'special' pony. Though he was only 13.2hh he often jumped in Junior Grade A classes, and we only missed qualifying for the Horse of the Year Show by one place. I was about twelve years old at the time.

"We only had one serious mishap, at the Stafford County Show, when I fell off and Arrow unluckily rolled on me. It was quite nasty and though I was only winded I thought I was dying. However I soon pulled myself together when I heard the ambulance arrive – and felt fine until the next day, when I went to the doctor. I almost fainted when he took out a needle to give me an injection!

"Apart from that, my only other serious fall from a pony was riding Tara. She took off a stride too early for a jump, with the net result that I ended up looking like a circus clown with a pair of lovely black eyes.

"The last pony I rode was, of course, that great trooper, Shipley Hills, owned by the Broome family. I was about fifteen and ready to move into horse classes. I was most upset to read a couple of years ago that he had died; but I suppose he was getting on. He was a terrific pony and we had a superb partnership. I'll never forget him!"

By the time she was 18 Lesley McNaught was already one of Britain's leading lady show jumpers.

Learning to Ride

One of the most common questions during a riding lesson is "Why bother about how I sit? Does it really matter as long as the pony goes?"

How much it does matter is obvious if you've ever given anyone a piggy back ride. If your passenger wriggles about, or leans too far forwards or backwards, it is very difficult to keep your balance, let alone to move in the right direction. Your pony is in exactly the same position, so the better you sit, the easier it is for him to cope with whatever is required. There is also the advantage that when dealing with a pony with problems (and bear in mind that many of them are caused by the rider in the first place) the better your position, the more effective you can be in sorting them out without having to resort to roughness.

Since you can't actually talk to a pony and expect it to understand you, your system of communication depends on a series of signals you give with your body. And only when you are sitting correctly in the saddle can you send the right messages.

Mounting and Dismounting

However basic it might seem, correct mounting and dismounting are as important as any other aspect of riding. In fact, if these are not done properly, you can cause a great deal of damage to the saddle – an expensive item to replace these days – as well as pain and perhaps irreparable harm to the pony's back. A pony that thinks it is going to be hurt each time the rider gets on can rapidly develop nasty habits which will make it difficult to mount and dismount safely.

Checking the girths

Before starting, check that the girth is tight enough; it should be possible to fit three fingers between it and the skin. Then gather up the reins in your left hand making sure they are both the same length and that there is a light contact with the mouth to prevent the pony moving forward. Take a handful of mane in your left hand to help reduce strain on the saddle. Face three-quarters on to the pony, looking towards the back of the saddle, then place your left

39

The correct way to mount. Make sure your pony always stands still.

foot in the stirrup iron, holding it steady with your right hand. Jump upwards as athletically as possible, turning to face the pony as you do so. As you go upwards, you can take hold of either the front of the saddle, or the far side of the waist with your right hand to help you balance. Never hold the cantle as this can twist the tree. Swing your right leg well clear of the pony's quarters, and then settle into the saddle – gently – not like a ton of bricks!

To dismount, take both the reins again in your left hand, place the right on the front of the saddle, remove both feet from the stirrups, and swing your right leg over the pony's back, making sure that you don't get it stuck behind the saddle. If you lean forward slightly, you'll find this easier to manage. So far I have assumed that you will be mounting from the near, or left hand side, but it doesn't hurt to become proficient at getting on and off from both sides, as it helps stop the pony from becoming one-sided.

HANDY HINT

To get your stirrup leathers roughly the right length before you mount measure them against your arm. With your knuckles on the stirrup bar the iron should reach up to your armpit.

Position

A good seat takes a long time to achieve, but although you should constantly work to improve it, it is important that you don't become stiff through trying too hard. You must also take conformation into consideration, both yours and the pony's; a broad backed pony, or a very narrow one, each create their own problems. Similarly, people born with long thin legs tend to have an advantage over those with shorter plumper ones! That isn't to say that a good classical position cannot be achieved by most people but some take more time and effort.

Once you have mounted and settled into the saddle, spend a few minutes sorting yourself out before asking the pony to move. You should be sitting as centrally as possible with your weight equally distributed over both seat bones. Viewed from the side, two straight lines can be drawn through the rider's body; so get somebody to watch and tell you when your seat is correct. The first line is a vertical one through the rider's ear, shoulder, hip and heel. The upper body should be upright, and you should be looking ahead. Length of stirrup depends on your experience; a novice will ride quite short until the riding muscles have loosened and stretched. A common mistake is to try to ride with too long a stirrup too soon: it will only put you off balance by making you tip forward and perch on the front of your seat.

Heels should be slightly lowered but not forced down unnaturally as this will push your lower leg away from the pony's sides.

The second straight line runs from your elbow, which should be resting against your side, along the forearm, wrist and rein to the pony's mouth. This allows your arm to be flexible and follow the motion of the pony's head. You should hold one rein in each hand with wrist and fingers flexed lightly and your thumbs on top of the reins.

This is the position you should try to adopt in all of the gaits, except when rising to the trot, or galloping. When riding fast you will probably need to shorten your leathers a hole or two, so that you can place more weight onto your knee and stirrups. Your upper body should move slightly forward from the hips, with the seat raised a little from the saddle, so that you can stay in balance with the pace, and allow the pony maximum freedom of movement in its back. In rising trot again take the weight onto your stirrups and incline the upper body forward. The movement will help to push you upwards and forwards in rhythm with the stride and this rising and sitting will help to stop both you and your pony from becoming over-tired during long periods in trot.

The more you can improve your position the better; as you grow more secure, so you will become more confident, and ready to ask for more from the pony.

This rider is sitting very well although the stirrup iron should be on the ball of her foot rather than her toe.

Left Walking *Right* Rising trot

The Aids

The "aids" are the signals you send to the pony by movements of your legs, seat, hands and body, telling it how fast and in which direction to move.

All horses and ponies are trained to move away from the pressure of your legs, so that if you close both of your legs gently but firmly on its sides, it should move straight forward. You will need to move your hands forward slightly to allow the pony to keep its balance by moving its head and neck. Prevent this movement, and the result is a bit like trying to drive a car with the handbrake on – it might possibly go, but not very well!

Once the pony has started to move, you will feel a gentle rocking movement in the walk and canter, and a somewhat bouncier one in trot. Your hips and waist should remain as supple as possible so that you can absorb the motion. Gripping with your legs should be avoided since it will stop you from sitting deep in the saddle, and you will end up being bounced around. A relaxed rider will always get more from any pony, and be able to be adaptable, which is particularly important if you can only ride at a riding school and are not always given the same pony.

To increase the pony's pace from walk to trot, you close your legs a little more strongly. Asking for canter is slightly diffe-
rent as the canter has a distinctive three time beat. The outside hindleg takes the first step, followed by the inside hind and outside foreleg together, and finally the inside foreleg. This gives the appearance of the pony taking a longer stride with its inside foreleg which is known as cantering on the correct leg.

The reasons for asking the pony to canter like this are obvious if you try a simple experiment for yourself. Run a small circle with first your inside, and then your outside leg taking longer strides. You will quickly discover which way round is easier to keep your balance!

To help achieve the correct leg when cantering, the pony's body should be bent slightly to the inside. The best place to ask for canter is at a corner or on a circle. Slide your outside leg back a little to prevent the pony from swinging its quarters outwards and losing the bend, and to ask the outside hindleg to take the first step into canter. Your inside leg is used on the girth as before.

In canter, the rider's weight should be a little further forward than in walking trot, to keep in balance with the pony's movements.

Slowing down differs slightly from increasing speed, although it needs just as much thought and preparation. Sit firmly down in the saddle, and instead of letting your hips rock with the movement of the pony's back, resist very slightly. At the same time, increase the pressure on the reins with your fingers. Remember to keep your legs lightly in contact with the pony's sides – otherwise instead of a nice active transition, you will get a rather abrupt braking!

Changing Direction

By using one leg more strongly than the other, you can move your pony both forwards and sideways. When you approach a corner, turn the pony's head slightly by moving your inside hand to the side; not backwards as that will only slow you down. Maintain the forward movement with your inside leg, whilst your outside leg is used more strongly to move the body after the head. If you slide the leg back a little as you use it, it will stop the quarters from swinging outwards, and keep them in a line behind the shoulders.

As you learn to apply the aids and become more conscious of your position, you will find you are also becoming more sensitive to the moods and way of going of each pony you ride. You will begin to feel a part of the pony rather than just another passenger. In other words you'll find you are developing that elusive equestrian instinct – a real "feel" for the pony you ride.

HANDY HINT

If you have to dismount and lead your pony it is a good idea to run the stirrups up the leathers so that they don't swing and bang against his sides. Take the reins over his head so that you have extra control if he is suddenly startled.

To turn to the left the rider has moved her outside leg behind the girth.

Your Pony's Tack

A visit to the saddler's can be a baffling experience. Rows and rows of shiny leatherwork, tangles of bits, mysterious straps and fittings; where do you begin?

As tack is probably the most expensive item on a pony owner's shopping list it is worth investing some time and effort when you come to choosing it. Not only that, well-fitting tack in good condition is essential for both yours and your pony's safety and comfort so bear this in mind when you are tempted to cut corners.

Some ponies may bring all the necessaries from their previous home but even so it is worth asking someone knowledgeable to check the tack, particularly the saddle, for fit and condition. A worn or damaged saddle can go unnoticed until a strap breaks at an untimely moment or a sore or injury appears on your pony's back.

Secondhand tack can be a big saving for the cost conscious pony owner but it is wise to buy it from a reputable saddler rather than a private seller. The saddler should not sell you tack which is dangerously worn and it is worth paying a little extra for this peace of mind.

The average pony and rider do not need expensive leatherwork, intricately stitched. On the other hand, don't go to the opposite extreme! The cheapest tack around is imported from India and although good saddlers will not stock it, you may come across it at sales or inherit it from your pony's last owner. Invariably this sort of equipment is shoddily made and unreliable and though it may seem a bargain at the time, will soon prove to be more trouble than it was worth.

The saddler at work

Saddles left to right: Dressage, general purpose with forward cut flaps, and show.

Buying a Saddle

When you remember how many hours you and your pony spend in a saddle you'll realize just how important it is that it should fit properly. Like a pair of uncomfortable shoes, a badly fitting saddle can pinch, rub and generally stop a pony performing at its best. But, it's not essential to buy a really expensive saddle, and some people actually prefer secondhand ones.

A good saddler will be happy to let you try several saddles to find the right fit. When you put a saddle on your pony, check first that it sits evenly on the back leaving a completely clear channel between the gullet and the pony's spine from pommel to cantle. If you stand at the withers and look under the front arch you should be able to see daylight at the other end!

It is sometimes quite a problem to find a saddle which is wide enough for broad ponies: if the front arch seems to perch, carry on looking, for although it may not be pressing down on the withers, it can still pinch the shoulders and spine. A saddle which rests on the withers will also damage your pony's back; ignore anyone who sug-gests that you should pad it with a numnah. It won't help at all.

The basic pony saddle will probably have a rigid tree which is the wood or fibreglass foundation on which the saddle is built. Look for one with a deep central seat and knee and thigh rolls to support your legs – this will help you to sit in the correct position. A spring tree saddle has steel insets for comfort and once you've ridden in one you'll find it hard (literally) to go back to a more basic type! Unfortunately they are also more expensive but if you're going to ride a lot, it might be worth saving up.

As you get more advanced you may decide you want to specialize and need a saddle to suit. Jumping saddles, for instance, have very forward cut flaps, excellent for jumping but less suitable when you lengthen your stirrups for everyday riding, and a dressage saddle has a much straighter cut with a deep seat to allow the rider to adopt a longer leg position.

If you're hoping to go in for showing classes – the riding pony beauty contests – then you'll need a special saddle which is straight cut to show off the pony's shoulder, and fairly flat in the seat to enhance the line of the back.

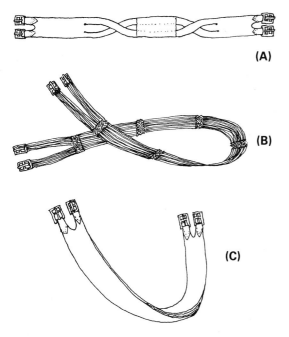

Girths: (A) Balding (B) Nylon (C) Three-fold

Girths and Stirrups

Your saddle will probably come "stripped" so you will need to buy the accessories to go with it. Nylon girths are cheap and fine for ponies as long as they are kept clean and checked regularly for fraying. They come in a variety of colours but white and brown generally look the most suitable. Show saddles require thin white web girths, two for safety. These look attractive but aren't very practical for everyday use.

The best kind of girths are leather but they are also the most expensive and must be kept supple or else they'll rub. The Balding divides into three crossing straps for extra comfort behind the pony's elbows. The Three-fold is also leather, folded around a piece of material soaked in oil to keep it soft. It should be buckled with the folded side lying next to the pony's elbow

and is beautifully soft if cleaned and oiled regularly.

Choose medium width stirrup leathers and always buy stainless steel stirrups as nickel, although cheaper, is an unreliable alloy which can crack or break even when brand new. The stirrup should be wide enough to allow a 1 cm gap at either side of the rider's foot, but not so big that the boot can slip right through. You can if you like fit rubber treads to your stirrups which some people swear keep their feet warm!

Cruppers and Breastplates

A crupper can be an absolute godsend for those cylindrical Thelwell-type ponies whose saddles always slip forward. It is a simple strap attached to the cantle of the saddle and running under the tail and it can save small riders from many embarrassing situations.

Breastplates similarly will stop the saddle sliding back but are generally only required for fast work such as racing, eventing or polo.

Numnahs and Saddle cloths

A numnah is a pad of foam or sheepskin, cut into the shape of the saddle and worn under it, supposedly to prevent pressure or chafing. In fact they are of very little use, as they can't improve an ill-fitting saddle and may even cause the pony's back to overheat. If your saddle is pressing on the pony's spine, then you should get it re-stuffed or change it for one which is a better fit.

Saddle cloths are just squares of material, purely decorative, and quite unnecessary, and can actually cause galls if they are put on carelessly.

If you ever have to tack up a pony which wears a numnah or cloth make sure it is pulled well up into the gullet of the saddle, otherwise when you sit in the saddle it will cause extra pressure on the pony's spine.

Bridles

There are three basic types of bridle: snaffle, pelham and double. The snaffle is the one you are most likely to use as it is the simplest and mildest, consisting of a single rein with a plain or jointed bit. When you are choosing one look for good quality medium width English leather. Bootlace thin bridles with stitched nosebands are very smart in the show ring but won't stand up to the rigours of everyday use.

There are lots of different kinds of reins to choose from and it is really a matter of personal preference. Nylon, though cheap and colourful, can stretch alarmingly. Plain leather or rubber-covered reins in a width which fits your hand comfortably are probably the best.

The bridle should fit easily around your pony's ears and allow room for three of your fingers under the throatlash, and two at the noseband. The bit should lie comfortably in the mouth, just touching the lips, and shouldn't bang against the teeth or be so big that it slips from side to side.

The pelham has a single bit with two reins. It incorporates the action of a snaffle with the stronger effect of the curb rein, which applies pressure via a curb chain, in the pony's chin groove. Occasionally you will see a pelham with leather roundings on the bit so that only one rein is used. Although this may be easier for an inexperienced rider to handle, it really cancels out the intended action of the bit.

The Kimblewick is a kind of pelham with just one rein. Like the pelham it has a curb chain which acts on the chin groove when the rider's hands are lowered. It can be useful for headstrong ponies as it has a stronger action than a snaffle but some ponies learn to lean on it and become very heavy in the hand if it is used regularly.

A double bridle has two bits, the snaffle and curb, which allow for more subtle and

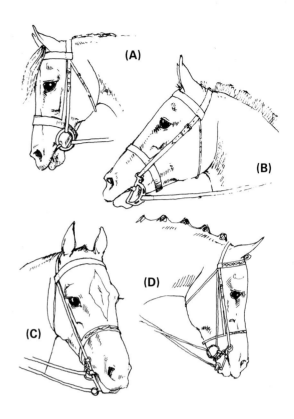

Bridles: (A) Snaffle
(B) Kimblewick (C) Pelham
(D) Double bridle

finely attuned application of the aids than just a snaffle. It is used for advanced training and in the show ring to enhance a well-schooled pony's balance and head carriage. However it should not be looked upon as a "brake" and is really only the province of an experienced rider.

Nosebands

Snaffle bridles can be fitted with a variety of different nosebands. A plain cavesson has very little influence on the rider's degree of control but a drop noseband can help to stop a pony crossing its jaw to evade the bit. A grakle or crossed noseband has the same effect but slightly stronger action.

Furry nosebands may look eyecatching but are best left to racehorses!

Above A running martingale can be useful on a headstrong pony.

Below Nosebands: (A) Cavesson (B) Drop (C) Grakle

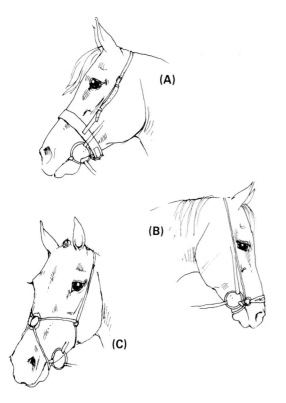

(A)

(B)

(C)

Martingales

Martingales are a supplementary means of control but should only be treated as a temporary measure and are not a substitute for basic schooling. Fastening at the girth, they pass between the pony's front legs to a neck strap. At this point the running martingale divides into two straps which attach to the reins. A standing martingale is fitted to a cavesson noseband.

The running martingale attached to snaffle reins and with a dropped noseband can be a great help when jumping the sort of "onward bound" pony which has a tendency to throw its head above the point of control. It may only be needed for jumping and as long as it is not adjusted too tightly (it shouldn't disturb the straight line of the rein between bit and rider's hand) it is a better answer than a more severe bit.

The standing martingale also helps to stop a pony throwing its head too high but some do learn to lean against it. It should only be attached to a cavesson noseband as otherwise it can interfere with the pony's breathing.

Headcollars

The smartest kind of headcollar is made of leather which, as long as it is cleaned regularly, will stay supple and shiny. Unfortunately it is also the most expensive, and nowadays nylon has become by far the most popular material. Nylon headcollars are easy to clean and don't deteriorate as quickly as leather if they are left covered in mud! Choose the most supple nylon you can find to reduce the risk of chafing and make sure it fits your pony properly. The noseband should fit like a cavesson and hang two finger's width below the cheekbones. You'll find they come in all sorts of colours – even Pony Club stripes – with leadropes to match so you can choose a colour co-ordinated set to suit your pony!

Nylon headcollars come in a vast range of colours. Choose one to suit your pony or match your jersey!

Rugs

Most native type ponies don't need much in the way of rugs unless they are living out in really cold weather. Then, along with clipped or thin-skinned ponies, they'll need a waterproof New Zealand rug to keep them warm and dry. There are lots of different patterns of New Zealand rugs to choose from, and your saddler will advise you on the best. Look for one which is tailored to fit, and add padding at the withers and breast if it is not already there. It is important that a New Zealand shouldn't slip when a pony rolls so to help keep them in place they have straps which cross between the hindlegs. These should be oiled regularly so they don't rub.

If your pony lives out all the time you will need two rugs. This is so that you can change them over every day to give the wet and muddy one a chance to dry out.

Clipped ponies will also need a stable rug made of jute, to keep them warm when they are inside. On cold nights, under-blankets can be added for extra warmth.

An anti-sweat sheet is a horsy string vest. It is used to help a pony dry out and cool down when it is sweating and should be fitted under a stable or travel rug to allow air to circulate. It is no earthly good using an anti-sweat sheet on its own – although plenty of people do! If you're using your stable rug over the anti-sweat sheet then turn it inside out so that the lining does not get damp.

Bandages

Most ponies will only need bandages for travelling. Stable bandages of thick wool should be placed over gamgee and should cover the pony's pastern and coronet. Alternatively you can use travel boots which have the advantage of being quick to fit as they are often fastened by velcro.

If your pony is doing a lot of jumping or fast work, your riding teacher might suggest you use exercise bandages to support the tendons. These are elasticated bandages, again fitted over gamgee, which should be applied quite tightly to the cannon bone area, from just below the knee to just above the fetlock joint.

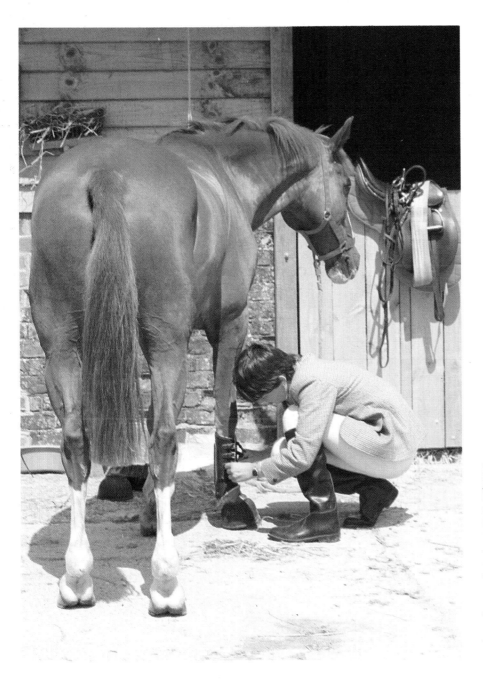

For fast work or jumping, protective boots are sometimes necessary. If a pony has a tendency to knock one foreleg against the other, known as brushing, he could actually lame himself. Leather brushing boots, fastened around the cannon bone and fetlocks, will guard against this.

Tack cleaning doesn't take long if you do it every day.

Care of Tack

Once you've got your tack it's important to take care of it as dirty leather soon becomes brittle and can crack easily. If you can bring yourself to do it, tack really should be cleaned every single time you use it. That way it is a ten minute job, otherwise you are letting yourself in for an hour of hard graft when your conscience finally catches up with you!

Start by undoing all the buckles on bridle and saddle and wiping off all the mud, sweat and grease with a sponge squeezed out in warm water. Don't soak the leather but do make sure it is clean before you go onto the next stage. There are various different kinds of saddle soap but one of the easiest to use is a glycerine bar. Dip one into water and rub it with a damp sponge then soap all the leather. If you make a lather, your sponge is too wet and it is best to dry everything off and start again.

Nylon girths, numnahs and rugs should be brushed clean; stirrups, buckles and bit rings can be polished, but keep metal polishes away from mouthpieces. Whilst you clean your tack make a habit of checking all the stitching and stress points for signs of wear and tear and get any dubious bits repaired immediately. It will prolong the life of your saddlery and could save you from a serious accident.

52

Learning to Jump

Whether you are interested in cross-country, showjumping or hunting, the thing to remember about jumping is that it should be fun for you and your mount.

It is important to start in the right way so that you both build up plenty of confidence; and even if you are already quite experienced it never hurts to go back to basics once in a while. An anxious rider can destroy the confidence of even the boldest pony and vice versa.

Having said that, the first question is, where to start?

Preparation on the Flat
The best basis for successful jumping is flatwork. Before you ever leave the ground, try to establish good even paces, with your pony moving with plenty of impulsion, and a good rhythm. Use serpentines and circles to improve suppleness, and make sure the pony is obedient to your leg; being able to lengthen and shorten the stride will help when it comes to jumping combinations and doubles. Do keep your work on the flat interesting and constructive, otherwise you will both get bored.

Trotting Poles
Once you have established the basic flatwork, you can begin your jumping lessons with single poles on the ground. As well as being a good introduction for pony and rider, trotting poles will encourage an experienced pony to "use" itself fully, and help to steady a fizzy, excitable animal.

Start by walking over a single pole, and then going over it in trot. If your pony tries to jump the pole, you will just have to be patient and persevere until he is going calmly.

The next stage is to scatter several single poles around your working area so that you can introduce changes of rein between them. This will also help to prevent boredom from setting in!

Having established this work, you can introduce a line of trotting poles. Never use just two poles as this can encourage a pony to jump rather than trot over them; three in number should be enough, placed four or five feet apart, depending on the length of your pony's stride. If possible, use painted poles which do not blend in with the ground, and encourage the pony to lower his head and neck and look at them. As you go over the poles, you should feel the trot becoming more powerful, as the pony has to pick his feet up a little higher and engage his quarters more.

At the same time, he will stretch out his head and neck and you should allow your hands to move forward slightly to follow this movement without losing your rein contact. If you pull your hands backwards or do not allow this stretching movement, you will upset the pony's balance. This would not be a major disaster over trotting poles, but would probably cause your pony to knock down a larger fence. The poles will work as an exercise not just for your pony, but also for you, teaching you instinctively to follow his movement, rather than snatching at the reins.

Practise your jumping position at a standstill.

Position

Another beneficial exercise is to practise your jumping position as you go over trotting poles. This will teach you to judge when to go forwards when it comes to the real thing.

On the approach to a jump, it is usually best to sit well down into the saddle, with a fairly upright position, so that you can maintain your rhythm and balance. This will help you to feel if the pony is going to stop at the fence, and to drive on more strongly if necessary.

As the pony takes off, you should stay as close to the saddle as possible, whilst going forward with his movement. You may be tempted to stand up in the stirrups but in fact the closer you can stay in contact with your mount, the safer you are going to be!

To help develop the correct position, practise this exercise: at a standstill, try reaching down and touching both toes with both hands at the same time. To do this you will find you have to move your hips back a little as your upper body comes forward, and keep your heels good and deep so that you don't lose your balance and can sit up again without holding your pony's neck. Shorten your stirrups a few holes from your flatwork length, and you will find it much easier. This is an exaggerated exercise but does give you a feel of the position you are trying to achieve when you jump.

Practise this crouching position as you ride over the poles but don't go quite as far forward (you are not jumping a six foot spread, remember!). Try to avoid the habit of leaning your hands on the pony's neck and instead let them move forward in line with the bit. The better you can keep your balance, the more help you will be to the pony, should it get into difficulties and jump awkwardly. Later on, there are all sorts of variations on this exercise, which you can use to improve your stability and position.

Jumping

For the moment though, back to basics!

Having mastered trotting poles, you can move on to a small fence. Introduce a small jump on the far side of the three trotting poles, at a distance of between eight and nine feet from the last pole. By a small

Trotting poles will encourage your pony to pick up his feet.

jump, I mean SMALL. There is no need to go overboard; something of about 1'3"–1'6" is usually quite high enough to give you the feeling of a jump without actually unseating you.

Approach in exactly the same way as you did when there was no jump. Try not to get anxious and over ride but at the same time look at the fence, not just the poles, or your pony may stop altogether! The poles will discourage any rushing, help to keep a lazy animal active and will also help to place the pony at the correct distance from the fence, so that it takes off neither too far away, nor too close.

Once you can·do this exercise quite happily, you can remove the poles, and after trotting over the jump, start to work over it in canter. It is a good idea to canter a circle before approaching the jump, so that the pace and rhythm are both well established first – a standing start from several yards away is *not* the ideal way!

If you get into difficulties and can't seem to approach and take off in the right place, put a canter placing pole in front of the jump, approximately eighteen to twenty-one feet away. This distance gives you time to canter over the pole and then room for one non-jumping canter stride to take off. It is important to get the pole right so that there is room to put in the extra stride; and if your pony tries to rush the fence, the pole is usually sufficient to steady him.

After all this practice over a single fence, try putting together a small course, so that you get used to riding on between the jumps; quite often the problems created are not by the obstacles themselves so much as the steering in between. Introduce plenty of variety where possible, so that jumping remains enjoyable and the pony does not become stale.

Show jumping is fun, but there is just as much pleasure in competently popping over a small log out hacking. Being able to enjoy your jumping does not necessarily mean riding at Wembley!

The Ghost in the Top Meadow

We had not lived at the Grange for long. It was an ideal place for us as it had six acres and stabling for eight horses. I was schooling in the top meadow when I first saw Philippa. I was attempting to ride a dressage test and everything was going wrong. Flicka simply would not walk and every few minutes her quarters would swing outside the arena I had marked with stones. As the rally for which I was schooling was less than a week away, I was beginning to feel desperate.

I had just dismounted and was shouting, "Will you stand still, you idiot!" when a female suddenly appeared from the hedge and standing a bare three yards away said, "Calm down. It's your fault. You're holding your pony too tight. Your stirrups are at least six inches too short, and your curb chain is twisted."

My mouth fell open with surprise as I stared at this apparition who spoke with such authority. Walking towards me, she continued in the same authoritative voice, "Turn your curb chain in a clockwise direction; it should lie comfortably in the chin groove. That's better. Now get up and let down your stirrups – you ride longer for dressage. Sit deep into your saddle." And she touched me with a hand lighter than a feather.

"Use your back and seat. Don't just wiggle your bottom," she said. "My God, you're terrible. You're just like a sack of potatoes. Now then, walk on, on a loose rein. Let your poor pony drop her nose and relax. That's better."

When she was more than a few yards away, I could no longer see her; but I could still hear her voice and it had a strange tone to it, like a voice in a dream. Yet it was not a dream but completely and utterly real.

And, amazingly, her instructions worked. Straight away Flicka improved, so that quite soon I was trotting round my pathetic arena without any trouble.

Soon she moved into the middle and started to shout instructions and sometimes I could see her and sometimes I couldn't.

"Change the rein," she called. "Now sitting trot. Prepare to halt. Sit down. Don't tug. Halt. What's your name?"

"Mark," I answered, trying to get her into focus, but seeing only bits of her, the edges but not the centre.

"Halt, Mark. That was terrible. Do you call that straight?" she shouted, coming into focus again. "Try it once more."

I could feel myself improving. Flicka felt different too, more relaxed and supple, she dropped her nose, her hindlegs were engaged and she had impulsion.

"That's enough for today," said my instructor suddenly. "Do you want another lesson tomorrow? You haven't much time, have you?" and she patted Flicka with a transparent hand and she actually seemed to like it.

"Yes please, if it's not too much trouble," I answered.

"Fine. My name is Philippa. See you tomorrow then. Same time, same place. And come in a plain eggbutt snaffle. You'll get extra marks for a snaffle and your pony doesn't need a pelham. And clean your tack; it's as stiff as cardboard." And with that she vanished into the hedge again, leaving my mind in a turmoil.

Riding back to the stable, I decided I would tell no one. The whole incident was so fantastic that no one would believe me anyway. They will think I'm mad, or spoil it somehow, I thought, dismounting. But I had not reckoned with my little sister Clare. She was in Flicka's manger playing with the kittens born three weeks ago.

"Who on earth were you talking to? I looked but I couldn't see anyone. It wasn't Flicka was it?" she asked.

"I was pretending I had an instructor," I lied, carrying my tack to the saddle room. "It helps me concentrate."

"I didn't know you could act so well! Perhaps you should be in the school play," suggested Clare. "I'll tell Mr Phipps."

"You dare," I shouted.

"Personally I think you're going bonkers," continued Clare, putting down the kittens. "Your eyes look funny, as though you've been seeing things. And you were talking like a woman."

"Just shut up will you?" I shouted.

The next lesson went even better. When it finished, Philippa said, "There's an old tennis marker in the bean shed. Put some whitewash or ceiling white on it and use it to mark out a proper dressage arena. The right size will be on your dressage sheet. We'll start doing bits of the test tomorrow and

perhaps some jumping. The day after, you'd better give Flicka a hack or she'll be getting stale. And remember to ride her up to the bridle whatever you're doing, and make her go straight."

I wanted to say, "Can I pay you?" or, "Come in for a drink," but I could not imagine her wanting either.

"Thank you very much," I said instead.

"Don't mention it. See you tomorrow, then." She patted Flicka and she looked pleased as though it was a very special sort of pat, and then she was gone.

This time Clare was leaning over the gate as I rode back to the stable. "Well, at it again. You even said thank you at the end. What's going on?" Her plaits were tight around her face and her voice was accusing.

"Nothing. Absolutely nothing," I said, riding past.

"I shall tell Mummy, or Daddy when he comes home from work. I shall tell them you are going bonkers," Clare called after me.

"You dare. You do and I'll kill you," I yelled and then, leaping off Flicka, I seized her plaits and twisted them round and round her head until she screamed.

"You dare," I repeated but without much conviction, because I knew I could not trust my little sister, that sooner or later she would tell someone and spoil everything.

I spent the afternoon marking out a dressage arena with the old tennis marker which Philippa had told me about. Mum was delighted that I had found something to do, that for once I was not loafing about getting on her nerves, or deafening her with my stereo system. Clare looked at me out of the corners of her small grey-green eyes, but remained silent.

I took my dressage test in my pocket for the next lesson and read it out loud to Philippa.

"Ah, much like the old test," she com-

mented. "We must concentrate on your transitions. You must not lose control as you change pace, one pace should glide naturally into the other."

"Are you pleased with the new arena?" I asked, looking past her to the hedge, behind which something was moving on all fours.

"Yes, it's wizard. Absolutely spot on," she answered, sounding gloriously old fashioned. "Are you ready? Try to enter straight. And remember, a nice bow to the judge with your hat off."

Flicka went marvellously. I had never known her go so well before. Even Philippa was pleased. "When is the great day?" she asked me as we finished the test.

"The rally is in three days' time. I would like to get selected for the Horse Trials team, but I don't suppose I will," I answered.

"Do not despair. Hack tomorrow; then we can run through the test the day before. That should do the trick," Philippa told me and for a moment I forgot that she was not quite real. "How about some jumping? There's the hedge and a nice little fence into the spinney," she suggested.

Years ago someone had made two jumping places in the long thorn hedge between the top meadow and the middle meadow and a little rail fence into the spinney. Flicka flew them, while Philippa called, "Steady. Keep her balanced. You're not going round the National. Well done," she said, as I stopped beside her. "Just remember to pull up your stirrups a couple of holes before you start jumping next time. You went round with a dressage seat. Goodbye." And she was gone again.

Clare met me by the field gate. There was a gleam in her eyes which I did not like. "I saw her over the hedge. I know your secret, Mark. I saw her with my own eyes. I want a lesson from your ghost, Mark. I need help, or I shall never pass C Test," she said, her eyes flashing, daring me to refuse.

"She's my instructor, not yours," I said.

"You can ask. You can't be that selfish," she whined. "And she's not your property, anyway, Mark."

"I'll think about it," I said, unsaddling.

If you knew my sister, her next remark would not surprise you: "If you don't, I'll tell Daddy, and that will put an end to it."

"Why not tell Mum as well," I said.

"I shall put an end to it," she repeated. "I don't know how, but I will."

And I knew she would. She's that kind of sister.

"All right. I'll see what I can do. But she's only a ghost and quite old so she may not want to take you on as well," I said.

My last lesson before the rally was fantastic. Everything went marvellously. At the end I said, "I'm awfully sorry to bother you, Philippa, but I was wondering whether you might be able to help my little sister too. She's hoping to pass C Test this summer."

Philippa laughed and floated to the hedge and back before saying, "I know all about C Test. Is she a nice girl?"

(And what could I say – "awful"?)

"Sometimes."

"I'll have a go then," she said.

"I wish we could pay you something," I told her. "I don't like putting upon you in this way."

"I don't want money. It is the root of all evil," she cried in a shrill, excited voice. "I hate the stuff. And what would I do with it? I don't need it, thank God."

"Thank you," I said. We were quite near one another now, so that I could see her more clearly than ever before. She was wearing the same clothes as she had when we first met. She must have died in them, I thought.

Then she raised a transparent hand with fingers like glass, waved and was gone.

Flicka behaved marvellously at the rally. There were congratulations all round.

"What have you done to her? She's fantastic," said one of my rivals. "Where have you been?"

"I've found a new instructor," I said.

"Tell. Tell us who."

"Not likely," I answered quickly. "She's fully booked."

I was selected for the Horse Trials team. Our District Commissioner congratulated me in person saying, "Your progress is astounding. I wish you could get your instructor to come here. We would pay whoever it is to be our team trainer."

"She's not interested in money. And she doesn't want any more pupils. She's old and she does it as a favour. Sorry," I said.

"What a pity. Try to make her change her mind, Mark. If she can help you so much in a week, she could improve this branch out of all recognition," continued our District Commissioner. "We would be champions within a year."

Two days later I was saying, "Philippa, this is my little sister, Clare," and Clare was muttering, "I'm not little."

"Oh, the one who wants to pass C Test. How do you do," said Philippa holding out her hand.

Clare kept her hands tight on her reins. She had no intention of shaking hands with a ghost. She had never seen Philippa so close before and her complexion had turned a shade paler. "What's it like being a ghost?" she asked.

Philippa ignored the question. Looking at Clare's dark brown pony, Holly, she said, "He's a Dartmoor, isn't he?"

"That's right," agreed Clare nervously.

"Your saddle needs stuffing. It's nearly on his withers. Take it to Mr Bradbury. He's a wizard saddler and he'll only charge you a fiver."

"Mr Bradbury? He's not there any more. He hasn't been for years. It's Paxton and Co. now and it will cost forty pounds. I know, because Mum asked," replied Clare, who is utterly devoid of tact.

"Shut up," I muttered. "Just shut up."

The lesson was the best I have ever had. Flicka had a wonderful slow canter now, as slow as her walk, or almost, and yet full of impulsion. I only had to close my fingers on the reins when I wanted to stop, or to close my legs against her sides to increase pace. It was more like magic than reality.

"I am so grateful," I said at the end of the lesson. "I simply don't know how to thank you."

"Don't then," Philippa said, floating away. "I enjoy it. I was always happy in this field."

"Whew, I'm stiff. I can hardly move," moaned Clare. "Do you think we'll look like her when we are dead? I couldn't shake her hand, I just couldn't."

"So I noticed. I think you were most ill-mannered. Poor Philippa, she looked very hurt," I answered.

"But there's no expression on her face," complained Clare. "It's like a mask, a pale, terrifying mask. So how could she look hurt?"

It might have gone on like that forever. I might have competed in the Badminton Horse Trials or represented Britain at the Olympics if Clare could have kept a secret. But Clare was only eleven, with masses of friends. She also liked doing good deeds as long as they were not too much bother, and she liked giving presents if she could get someone else to pay for them. So it was not long before she was offering Philippa's instruction to all her friends. I tried to stop her. I ranted and raved and called her unrepeatable names, but to no effect.

"You must come," she told her nasty little friends. "She's a ghost and it's absolutely free." And of course they came in droves for who could resist such an invitation – free instruction *and* a ghost?

I was furious, but Philippa seemed to enjoy it. "I love a big class," she said. "But not more than twelve, more than that is counter-productive."

Presently there was a waiting list and I suppose it was inevitable that before long parents would start asking about such an amazing instructor.

No one knows who actually spilt the beans; but on a muzzy September day, when the top meadow was speckled with mushrooms and the hedges purple with blackberries, the end came.

Afterwards I blamed myself. I wept. I shook Clare until her teeth rattled and her face turned purple. I slammed doors and locked myself in my bedroom and tore my riding shirt to shreds. I could not eat. I wanted to die. For two terrible days I went berserk, but Philippa never returned.

There were twelve riders in the class that day, nearly all female, their eager faces pink with pleasure under their peaked riding caps, their ponies cleaner than they had been in years. They kept pushing inwards the better to see Philippa and at intervals they giggled shrilly, rather like delighted birds descending on an unexpected harvest of food.

I do not know exactly when someone's parents first appeared with a keen newspaper man in tow. No one had asked permission. I just became aware of spectators by the gate and felt the hair stand up along my spine. They could not see Philippa yet. The younger riders were practising the turn on the forehand with Philippa waving a transparent hand, her face lit by some unearthly inner light, so that it glowed visibly like a lantern.

"Well done!" she cried enthusiastically.

"You get better every time. Just a little more impulsion as you halt."

Seeing the strangers, I was overcome by an appalling sense of doom. I wanted to shout, "Go away, what are you doing here?" but so great was the feeling that I was rendered speechless.

So they advanced chattering, insanely normal, like people going to a party, the newspaper man oozing eagerness like a terrier scenting a rabbit. What a story! shining all over his ruddy face.

When I found words, they were too late, for they had reached Philippa's orbit by then and the newspaper man was priming his camera, and then adjusting the filter with a hand shaking with excitement.

"Don't!" I shouted. "Please don't."

But too late, for at the same moment he pressed a switch and there was an enormous flash, and Philippa fell like a heap of clothes on a stick. There was nothing where she had stood but charred earth, and I knew with awful certainty that this was final, that now she was really dead for ever and ever, and that she would never come back again.

I leapt from Flicka like someone possessed and seizing the camera flung it on the ground and jumped on it screaming, "You've killed her. Are you satisfied now? She's dead! She'll never come back!" Tears were streaming down my face.

And the silly children who had caused it all started to scream and cry and turn for home . . .

"Stop it, Mark, stop it," cried my mother

who had appeared, alarmed by the noise, for now I had the newspaper man by the throat. "What's the matter? What's come over you?" she shrieked. Then someone led me to the house as though I was mentally ill, while another led Flicka to the stable, and I kept saying over and over again, "They've killed her! She was the best instructor I ever had and they killed her!"

It took me a long time to recover. For weeks I could not bear to enter the top meadow, for days Flicka remained bored and unridden, and I spoke not a word to Clare. But time heals all and odd to relate some six weeks later when I was in the forge watching Flicka shod, I heard the story of Philippa. Flicka was having a hind shoe nailed on when a bent old man entered the forge and looking at me, said, "So you are the young man I keep 'earing about. The one who's been 'aving lessons from Miss Philippa, who's walking around with a broken 'eart, or so they're saying at The Coach and Horses."

"Yes. But she's dead now, and she won't come back," I replied mournfully.

He looked at me with a twinkle in his eye and said, "And you wouldn't be the first 'eart she's broken. What a girl she was! She 'an 'er sisters had stables at your place, you know. They started with nothin', built it up from scratch like. What girls they were; but she were the star, weren't she Frank?" he asked, addressing the blacksmith who would never see fifty again.

"Yes, we always called her the boss; she ran it," he said.

"They had forty 'orses you know. There was a lot more stabling then and they rented all the paddocks around. Oh, the village was different then, full of colour it was," the old man continued, his eyes brightening as he talked.

"The other two married, but Philippa stayed on. She could ride anything, you know, train it perfect, all done by kindness too. But it was an 'orse what killed her in the end. She couldn't stop working, you know, and she wasn't well at the time; she was just getting over pneumonia, wheezing terrible she was." The old man was sitting on a bench now, his gnarled hands clasped between his knees. "She took an 'orse no one could ride to the top meadow. She 'ad 'im on the lunge, see. No one knows what really 'appened but they found 'er with the rein tangled round 'er neck and the 'orse standing over 'er and they swore the 'orse was crying. 'E never gave any more trouble, but she was dead. You should 'ave seen the funeral. You couldn't get in the church for people. They came from miles away, and the village 'as never been the same since. She was only forty, you know."

"Thank you for telling me," I said. "I knew she was the sort of person you meet only once in a lifetime. I miss her unbearably and I only knew her for a short time."

"Perhaps she's at rest now," the Blacksmith said, looking at my anguished face. "Perhaps it's better that way. No one should go on working when they're dead."

"But she loved it. She was so happy," I answered. And I had to look away and blink back my tears.

Grooming and Pony Care

"Why do ponies need grooming anyway?" you may ask, as the rain pelts down the window and the stable seems an uninviting prospect. "Wild ponies don't." The simple answer is that wild ponies live in quite different conditions from domesticated ones. They need the grease in their coats to protect them from bad weather. They don't wear shoes so their hooves are kept in trim naturally as they range around their territory looking for food. They probably have fleas or lice but there is no rider to mind that.

The way you groom and care for your pony depends very much on how he is kept and the sort of work you do with him.

A Grass-kept Pony
A pony which lives out all year round doesn't need much grooming at all. This is because he needs the natural greases in his coat to protect him from the rain and cold; it is his form of waterproofing. However, you can't just push him out into the field and forget about him in between rides. He will need to be caught and checked over every day and tidied up before you put a saddle on his back.

If your grass-kept pony is shod you will have to pick his feet out each day. Work from heel to toe with your hoof-pick and at the same time, check down his legs for cuts and behind his heels for cracking or sores caused by the mud. Keep an eye on his shoes to make sure they don't become loose or worn and run your hand around the outside of his hoof and see if any of the nails are sticking out. These are known as risen clenches and it means he is due for a trip to

the blacksmith; torn or overgrown horn is another sign that he needs re-shoeing.

In winter especially, grass-kept ponies spend most of their time looking like muddy hearthrugs. Their long coats keep them warm but make it extra difficult for you to clean them up before a ride. A New Zealand rug will help immeasurably to keep the worst of the mud off their backs, otherwise you'll have to resort to some hard work with a rubber curry comb and dandy brush.

A rubber curry comb will help to loosen the dirt on even the muddiest pony.

Starting at your pony's near (left) side, work methodically from head to tail using firm circular movements with the curry comb to dislodge dirt. Be careful not to knock and hurt the pony in your enthusiasm and avoid prominent bones like his hips or the thinly covered joints of his legs.

65

You may be tempted to use a metal curry comb on the worst of the dirt but don't; these are for cleaning body brushes – not ponies!

It may be impossible to get your pony completely clean in the middle of winter so concentrate on the parts of his body where the tack will rest. Mud underneath the girth for instance, can soon cause chafing and galls if it isn't brushed off.

Although it is strictly frowned upon you may find you have to use the dandy brush on your pony's mane and tail as well. Ideally you should only use a soft body brush as the coarser bristles of the dandy can split the hairs – but when the choice is between that or a tail solid with mud, I think you have to choose the lesser of the two evils!

In the spring and autumn ponies "cast" or change their coats which means that your dandy brush will get clogged up with lots of loose hair. A rubber curry comb really comes into its element here and can be easily "emptied" by tapping on a fence or the floor.

In the summer when the weather is milder you can spend a little more time on your pony as the greases in his coat will not be so necessary. However, it is still best not to polish him *too* hard unless you are going off to a show.

In the height of the summer you'll probably notice lots of little yellow specks on your pony's legs. These are bots' eggs and are very difficult to brush off. But if you leave them, they'll end up in your pony's stomach and do him no good at all so it is worth five minutes work with your fingernails to make sure you get rid of them all.

The Stable-kept Pony

A pony who lives in a stable most of the time and is only turned out for a few hours in winter, snug in a New Zealand rug, needs quite a different regime from the outdoor types.

Grooming will remove the grease from his coat, brushing the natural oils through the hairs to make them shine and toning his muscles at the same time. It will help to keep him healthy – and smart.

Grooming kit. Body brush; leather pad for wisping; cactus cloth for polishing; dandy brush; mane comb; hoof pick; metal and rubber curry combs.

If your pony wears rugs indoors, perhaps because it is winter, and he has been clipped, then he will need tidying up in the morning and evening when they are changed or straightened.

After his daily exercise he should be groomed in earnest which is known as strapping. Strapping a pony properly should take about half an hour – and leave you feeling pretty tired!

Start by removing any mud or sweat with the dandy brush. Go carefully, as some stabled ponies may be very thin-skinned and sensitive, especially if they've just been clipped. A dandy brush might be too harsh to use on their coats and if this is the case go straight on to the softer brush.

The main work of strapping is done with the soft bristled body brush. Start at your pony's head on his near side and brush his mane out carefully, lock by lock. Then, throwing it over to the far side and holding the brush in your left hand, brush down his crest in long sweeping strokes. Work down his shoulder and foreleg then along his body to his quarters, pausing every three or four strokes to run the brush through a metal curry comb held in your right hand. You might have to change hands to groom your pony's belly and hindlegs; you'll certainly need to when you change sides.

When you get to your pony's tail, dispense with the curry comb and, standing just to one side of his quarters, holding the tail in one hand, brush the tail out a little at a time until it is tangle-free.

By now your pony should be shining, and your arms aching! To add the finishing touches you could polish his coat with a stable rubber or wisp him.

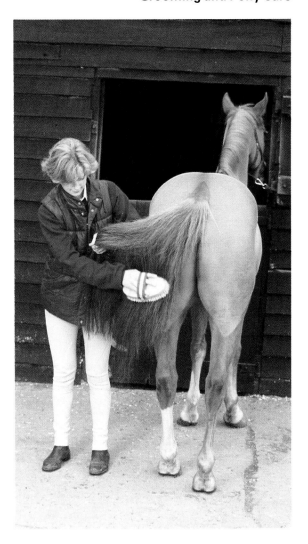

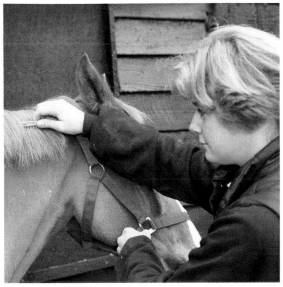

Above Stand at right-angles to your pony's quarters when brushing tail.
Right Combing a pulled mane

Wisping is a wonderful way to tone up muscles – yours as well as his! It involves banging the well-muscled parts of the neck, shoulders and quarters with a pad of hay or folded stable rubber. Get someone to show you how to wisp properly, as a lot hinges on rhythm and making sure you hit the right muscles. Never, for instance, wisp a pony over its loins as you could damage the internal organs which lie just below the skin.

Wisping makes the most awful thumping noise but funnily enough ponies seem to quite like it. My own pony used to close his eyes and sway in time to the rhythm!

All that remains now is to clean your pony's eyes, nose and dock (using separate sponges) and to pick out his feet. You could add some hoof oil to make him look smart and help to keep the horn in good condition.

Trimming

If your pony lives out most of the time he will need his mane and tail, untrimmed, to protect him from the weather. But in the summer, you will probably need to tidy him up a little, especially if you are planning to go to a show.

It is a great mistake to cut a pony's mane with scissors as this makes it look rather blunt and peculiar. The best way to trim a mane is by *pulling*, combing up the shorter top hairs a lock at a time and pulling out the long underneath hairs with a quick jerk. It is a good idea to get someone to show you how to do this, then you can keep your pony's mane neat by taking out just a few hairs as they grow too long.

A properly pulled mane looks neat as it is, but if you are going to a show you may decide to plait it, to look extra smart. Neat plaiting is an art so again, persuade someone to give you a demonstration and practise a few times before the big day.

Sponging nostrils and dock

68

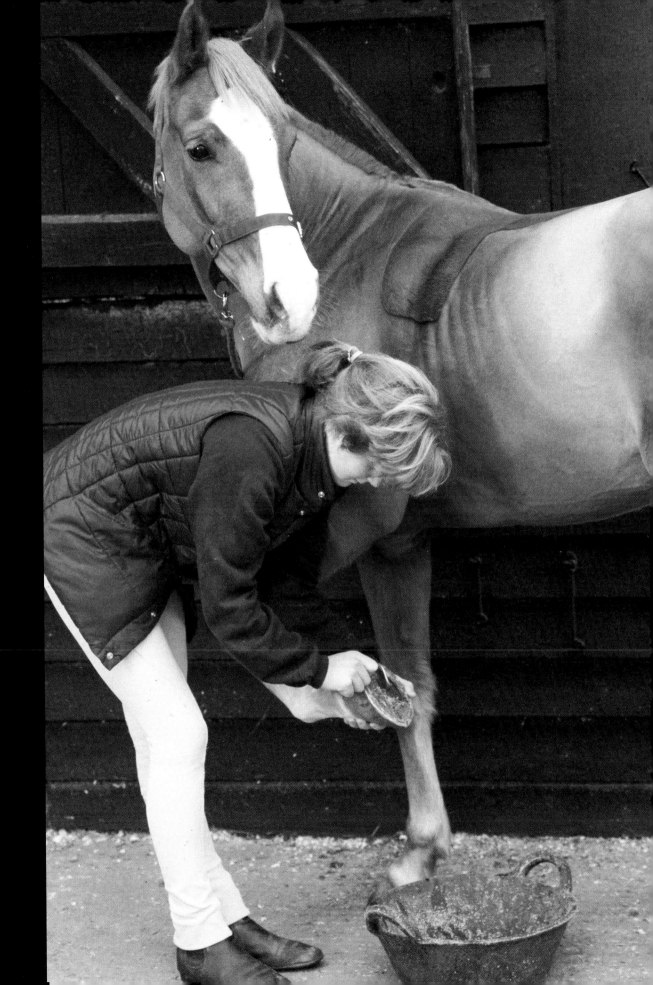

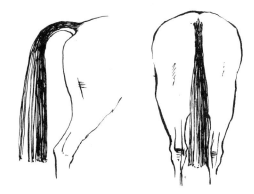

(A) Pulled tail trimmed straight below the hock

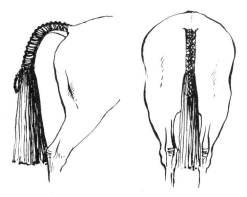

(B) A thick or bushy tail can be plaited for a show

HANDY HINT

Trying to keep your pony's tail clean for a show? After you've washed it, slip into a stocking and put a tail bandage on top – but don't forget to take it off before you go in the ring!

Your pony's tail can be trimmed quite easily by cutting it straight across the bottom. Ask someone to hold the tail out slightly, which is the way it will hang as your pony moves, and then cut it to just below the hocks. Pulled or plaited tails are smart for the show ring, and again will take a little time to perfect.

If your pony is a purebred Mountain and Moorland or Arab then his mane and tail should be left in its natural state for showing. The same applies to his "feathers", the hairs which grow at his heels. Otherwise you can trim these with scissors and comb or clippers. It is rather unfair to trim the long hairs around the pony's muzzle and eyes as he uses them as "feelers". However you can trim his ears by gently "folding" them and using nail scissors to cut off the fluffy bits of hair which stick out!

If your pony has a very thick or bushy mane you could also cut a "bridle-path" behind his ears – an inch wide "clearing" in the mane which allows the headpiece to lie snugly. Watch out though that your bridle-path doesn't get a little bit wider every time you trim it, otherwise it will start to look unsightly.

To plait a mane, dampen and separate into sections. Plait each lock, secure at bottom with needle and thread, roll tightly up to the neck, and sew securely into place.

Clipping

In the winter you'll see quite a lot of clipped ponies around, especially if they are expected to work hard, either hunting or in riding schools. Clipping involves removing some of the pony's thicker winter coat to help prevent him from sweating and make him easier to clean and dry off.

If a pony is clipped he'll probably need to wear rugs – a waterproof New Zealand in the field and a stable rug inside. The best kind of clip for a pony is the *trace clip* which trims his coat down his throat, chest and belly, the areas where he is likely to sweat the most. A *hunter clip*, for a pony in really hard work, leaves only the saddle patch and possibly the legs unclipped, but it does mean the pony will need rugging up well in the stable and field.

Clipping should be done by an expert but it is usually quite easy to find someone to oblige at a local riding school or livery stable. The first clip should be made in the autumn with one or two more through the winter depending how quickly the pony's coat grows.

A hunter clip

A trace clip

HANDY HINT

An uneven number of plaits along a pony's neck will make it look more elegant than an even amount. To help you work out the right number, divide the mane up into equal sections with elastic bands before you sew in the plaits.

Schooling Your Pony

You don't have to wait until you are training for a competition to bother about schooling your pony. Even if you only want to hack, a few short schooling sessions each week will give you a more supple, pleasant and obedient ride. It's no fun anyway to ride a pony which pulls your arms out the whole time or won't canter when you want to; and if you are preparing for a competition then a sensible schooling plan should improve the results.

Apart from producing a more enjoyable ride, schooling can also stretch the mind a little as well as the muscles. The more variety you can introduce into your riding the better, as it is often through boredom that evasions begin.

Working Area

When the word "schooling" is mentioned some people look a bit blank, as they aren't sure what it involves or how to start. Basically, you are aiming to improve the general manner in which your pony goes, and to do this you can use a variety of schooling exercises.

First of all, though, you need somewhere to ride and if you aren't lucky enough to have access to an indoor school or manège, you must mark out your own working area.

Plastic cones or small oil drums can be set around your rectangular school and painted with letters. These, starting clockwise, at the top end of the school, should read A, K, E, H, C, M, B, F – the markers used in a dressage arena.

The size of the arena wants to be roughly 20 × 40 metres, with the oil drums spaced out as accurately as possible. It is sometimes a good idea to site your homemade manège deliberately close to other horses in stables or fields so that your pony gets used to working with distractions.

Warming Up

Begin your schooling session with a little bit of time spent warming up. This will give you a chance to limber up as well as your pony, and to check over your position. Spend the first few minutes in walk on a long rein so that the pony starts the lesson in a mentally and physically relaxed state.

Once you have taken up the contact, introduce some changes of rein. This means, quite simply, changing the direction in which you are riding round the school and will stop the pony from becoming bored or stiff. The simplest changes of rein are down the centre line (AC or CA), across the breadth of the school (EB or BE), or by turning diagonally across the school (MK, KM or FH, HF). Later you can make these changes more interesting and demanding by riding two half circles across the school or describing a figure **S** shape.

Left You can make your own schooling arena with lettered markers.
Right Some of the different ways of changing the rein or direction inside an arena. The simplest is across the diagonal, as it allows room for a wide turn.

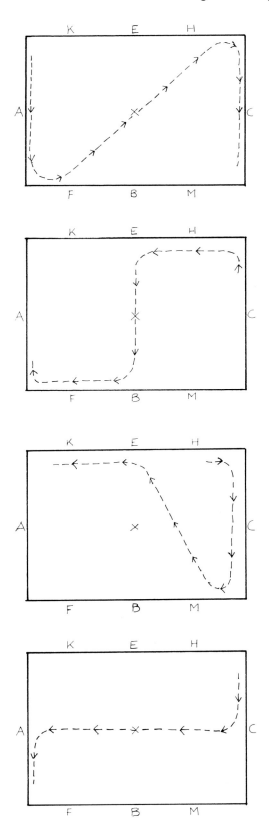

Changes of Pace

Changing the pace also helps to prevent boredom setting in and will improve your pony's balance and activity. A series of rapid transitions from walk to trot, halt, trot, then walk again can work wonders, especially with a slightly "stodgy" pony, by waking it up and getting it on its toes.

Two of the most useful movements to ride when schooling are circles and serpentines. At their most basic almost any novice pony can perform them but they can be adapted to make them more difficult as you both advance. They are excellent suppling exercises but must be ridden as accurately as possible, otherwise you won't get the maximum benefit from them.

Circles

The largest and easiest circle to ride in the confines of your working area is 20 metres in diameter starting from the A, E, C or B markers. If you have trouble gauging the size of your circle, mark out its four tangent points with stones as a guide. A twenty-metre diameter circle starting at A for instance, will pass through a point on the track halfway between E and the corner, X (the centre of the school), then to the track again halfway between B and the corner, finally returning to A.

Your pony should curve in the direction of the circle with an even amount of bend along the length of its spine. If it is stiff,

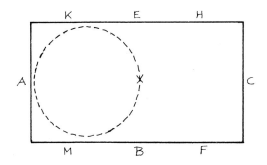

A 20-metre circle is easiest to ride.

however, it may bend too much in the neck so that it can swing its quarters or shoulders outwards and avoid having to use its back.

It is not hard to connect this problem with napping, where a pony will refuse to move in the desired direction by using exactly the same tactics. A pony like this is described as being rubber-necked, and can make life a misery when you want to circle accurately, or ride away from other horses. You can usually overcome problems by using your outside aids more firmly; the outside leg well drawn back to keep the bend in the spine, and a firm contact on the outside rein to prevent too much neck bend, and to stop the outside shoulder escaping. Check that you do not pull back on the inside rein; you should be able to see the pony's inside eyebrow – no more. The curve in the pony's ribcage and his forward impulsion should be encouraged by your inside leg on the girth.

The size of the circles you ride can be adjusted according to the ability of your pony. The smaller the circle, the more difficult it is! Once you reach ten-metre diameter circles, it is best to ride in a sitting rather than rising trot, as it gives you greater control and enables the pony to balance himself better.

Circles encourage the pony to use his back as he has to stretch the muscles on the outside and shorten those on the inside in order to bend. They also help to make his hindquarters more active.

Many ponies tend to "go on the forehand"; in other words, they place most of their weight on their shoulders and forelegs, which is easy for them but also makes them rather unbalanced. It can also be very tiring for the rider as the pony will often lean on the rider's hands. Regular schooling will make the hindlegs work much harder so that the pony begins to support itself more evenly instead of overloading the forehand.

Circling during a class lesson

It will make riding more pleasant for yourself, as well as giving the pony the chance of a longer working life.

Circles can also help to steady a pony which rushes and is "above the bit". This is the opposite problem to "going on the forehand" as the pony hollows its back and pokes its nose in the air. Ponies that are habitually "above the bit" are easily recognizable by the large bulge of muscle that forms on the underside of the neck! It makes for an uncomfortable and often rather uncontrollable ride. Too much speed is frequently the cause and plenty of circles will enable you to slow the rhythm down without loss of activity.

Circles can become very monotonous as well as tiring for a stiff pony so alternate them by changing rein and "going large", in other words, riding around the full track of your school. Work evenly on both reins to keep your pony's muscles supple and relaxed.

HANDY HINT
Wellingtons are dangerous for riding as the treads can get trapped in the stirrup, similarly plimsolls can slip straight through. Riding boots or strong low-heeled shoes are best.

In really cold weather, wear tights under jodhpurs – jockeys do!

Schooling Your Pony

Serpentines

Serpentines are a little more complicated than circles as they involve several changes of bend. Basically, they are a series of loops which can be either shallow ones to either side of the centre line or much deeper, taking in the whole breadth of the school. The latter are easiest to start with as they give you more time to straighten the pony and sort out your aids between changes of bend.

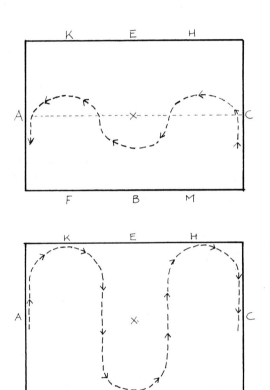

Two types of serpentine

Serpentines are a very good way of determining the stiffer and suppler sides of the pony. A "one-sided" pony which favours one rein much more than the other can be improved by riding a small circle in each loop of the serpentine. This will give you some extra time in which to establish the bend properly before straightening and riding on to the next loop and change of bend.

Markers will help you to ride accurately.

You can invent endless variations for yourself using these two basic movements and if they are ridden accurately they will make your pony more supple, active and balanced.

As you spend more time schooling your pony, you should find you develop a closer relationship, and learn a lot more about his personality – an added bonus to the improvements to your riding.

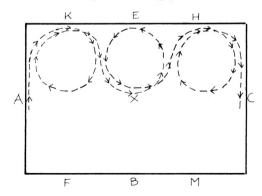

Stable Tricks and Tips

Ponies can be the most affectionate animals you could ask for: they'll whinney when they see you approach, nuzzle you softly, and put up with hours of patting and pampering; they can also be the most cunning and annoying.

Far more than horses, ponies will "take advantage" if you are not very experienced, and develop a whole repertoire of irritating tricks and habits which are quite liable to drive you up the wall. However, just as with naughty children, unless a pony is a confirmed delinquent, firm but sensible handling will cure most problems.

Here are some of the likeliest tricks you'll come up against, and some hints to set them right.

Hard to Catch

If this is your pony's failing you will probably know the scene quite well. You walk right across the field to your grazing pony, clutching your bridle so that you can tack him up and take him off for a ride. He watches you approach out of the corner of his eye then, just as you're a hair's breadth away, he whisks around and trots annoyingly to the farthest possible corner!

First of all, don't underestimate the power of tempting titbits. A rustly bag or clanky bucket may be all that's needed to attract his attention (although be careful you don't find yourself surrounded by every other horse in the field). You are also far more likely to be successful if you approach

your pony slowly, calling his name, so that he knows you're coming, and hiding the headcollar behind your back. Run up behind him swinging your tack, and you are very likely to startle him.

You could also try leaving his headcollar on when he is turned out so that you have some purchase when you come to catch him, but be sure it fits properly and cannot chafe or snag.

A pony who is ridden every time he is caught will quickly learn to associate you with work and decide his field is preferable, so try to vary your routine. Make a habit of catching him whenever you take him feed or water, pat or groom him and then turn him out again.

If you have a serious problem with a pony you can't even secure at feed times, try taking a book into the field, sitting down by his feed – and waiting! Eventually greed or curiosity will overcome even the wildest pony and he will decide to investigate. It may take days or even weeks but perseverance will pay off in the end!

Difficult to Bridle

It is not really surprising that some ponies are difficult to bridle. Imagine a cold, heavy piece of metal being banged against your teeth and tight leather straps being pulled over your ears. It is important to be as gentle as possible when you tack up your pony so that you don't make difficulties for yourself in the future.

Many ponies find they can avoid bridling simply by sticking their noses in the air. This can pose quite insuperable difficulties if you have short legs – and an upturned bucket is not really the long-term solution!

Obviously it is easier to bridle a pony in a stable as this imposes its own restrictions on his mobility. When you tack up, position him in a corner so that he can't reverse away from you. Starting with the bridle, place

the reins over his head, just behind the ears. This will give you a certain amount of control and keep the reins looped safely out of the way.

Standing on your pony's near side slip your right hand under his chin to take hold of his nose quite firmly. Gather the bridle into this hand and cradle the bit on your left. Now comes the tricky bit. Your pony will probably clench his teeth so stretch your thumb up to the corner of his lips and push it into his mouth. There is a gap in his teeth here which means he can't bite you but it will make him open his mouth. You must slip the bit in quickly, sliding your right hand up his face and taking up the slack in the cheekpieces so he can't spit it out again. Slip the headpiece over the ears and the rest is plain sailing!

A pony who is very headshy may be more amenable if you undo the near side cheekpieces so that you can put the headpiece on first and then slip the bit in from the side. However, if you aren't very experienced you may find that you get inextricably tangled; so don't try this unless you are sure you can buckle the bridle back together!

Won't Pick Up Feet

A young pony may genuinely not understand what you want to do, but there are plenty of older ponies who will sink their weight quite purposely onto the foot you are trying to pick up!

If you think the pony may kick, stand up close to him with a friend holding his head. Starting at his shoulder or hip run your hand down the leg until you reach the fetlock. Now, lean against the leg and tug briskly at the tuft of hair at the back of the fetlock. If this doesn't work, pinch the skin gently and as the foot comes up, cradle the hoof in your hand. Don't just let go when you've finished as this will jar the hoof, startle the pony and make him less obliging next time. Lower the foot gently and give him a pat.

Kicking Doors

Ponies kick stable doors because they want attention. Perhaps they are bored, or maybe they can hear you mixing their feed. Whatever the reason, it's an annoying habit that can damage doors – and hooves! As ponies are terrible copycats, if one door-kicker joins the yard the rest will soon join in and before you know it you will find yourself with a stable full of percussionists! Bearing in mind that the pony probably keeps on kicking because he enjoys the noise, the first step is to spoil the effect. This can be done quite successfully by lining the door with rubber matting or sections of car tyre. Providing alternative entertainment can also help; a salt lick on the wall or turnip in a feed bucket might be just the "toy" that's needed. Finally, ask yourself whether your pony is really bored rigid and if you can't give him more exercise think seriously about altering his regime so that he can be turned out for longer periods.

Bed Eating

Some ponies seem to have a permanent weight problem. As soon as you reduce their hay or cut down their grazing they look for other forms of nourishment and diversion, and that usually means they set about eating their beds. Just about the only way to discourage a pony from eating straw is to sprinkle the bedding with diluted disinfectant after you have mucked out. However, nowadays wood shavings and shredded paper are becoming quite popular alternatives and it may be worth considering these if your pony is a confirmed glutton.

Won't Stand Still

One of the most irritating things a pony can do is set off gaily for a ride while you're still halfway into the saddle. At best you land in an ungainly heap on top, clutching for reins and stirrups; at worst, you hop desperately after him, one foot wedged in the stirrup and the saddle slipping slowly round. You can easily end up flat on your back.

It's a habit a pony usually learns as a youngster, from a rider who is always in too much of a hurry to insist that he stands still. How many people do you know who are quite proud of the way they can swing carelessly into the saddle as their mount makes for the open road?

The cure, you'll be pleased to know, is quite simple; the snag is that it may require literally hours of perseverance! Whenever it is time to mount up, stand your pony beside a fence or facing a wall so that he can't swing away from you. Holding your reins quite short, place your left foot in the stirrup and if he moves as much as a hoof, take it out again until he is still. Repeat the whole process, over and over again until the pony will stand quietly whilst you mount and wait for your signal to move off. Never give in, however much of a hurry you are in, and make sure you insist every single time you get on. It will pay off in the end, I promise!

Won't Load

When you think about it, it is surprising more ponies don't make a fuss about travelling. They are packed into dark, narrow rattly trailers or boxes, which sway around corners and stop and start unexpectedly. Once they reach their destination, usually a show, they have to work all day, then face a return trip.

However, ponies are generally obliging souls and don't make a fuss about loading up unless they've had a particularly nasty

scare – or think they can pull your leg!

The basic rules for easy loading are as follows. Firstly, be firm. March your pony up to the ramp as if you mean business. If you're expecting trouble, lead a friend of his in front to give him confidence. A haynet and some pony nuts will help to bribe him inside and if you have a trailer with two ramps you could try opening the "front door" to make it lighter and more inviting. But be careful your pony doesn't whizz straight through!

If the pony really digs in his heels at the foot of the ramp, ask two friends to walk up behind him holding a leadrope or lunge rein between them. The rope around his quarters will encourage the pony to move forwards whilst the assistants on either side should stop him swinging out.

A variation of this idea for a really stubborn pony is to attach two lunge reins to the sides of the trailer. The assistants, holding a rein each, cross behind the pony so that he is channelled up the ramp.

Of course it is important that a pony has lots of protection in a trailer, so that he doesn't get hurt. Thick bandages or travel boots are a must, as is a tail bandage because ponies tend to rest on their tails to balance themselves in transit. Ask your driver to go gently round corners and to brake and accelerate smoothly – then your pony will have less reason to complain about loading!

HANDY HINT

Speak to a pony as you approach him in a stable or field. If you creep up behind him even the quietest pony may be startled and kick out.

81

Feeding Ponies

Ponies are naturally grazing animals. In their wild state they live in herds which are constantly on the move, searching their territory for the best sources of water and food. Domestic ponies however are totally dependent on their owners to keep them alive and well. This is a big responsibility for pony owners and to avoid making any bad mistakes and be sure you are doing the best for your pony, it is important to take the feeding seriously.

The Grass Fed Pony

Ponies which live out are obviously in a more natural environment than those living in stables, However, the pony's search for food and water is still restricted to his paddock or field so in terms of providing a correct diet, keeping a pony at grass is not quite as simple as it sounds.

There are several important things to consider:

- Is the size of the field suitable for the pony? This will depend on the type of grazing available and the number and kind of other animals sharing the land.

- What is growing in the field? This obviously changes throughout the year. Spring and summer grazing is the best and whilst some ponies thrive on this, others which get fat easily can contract laminitis, a very painful complaint of the foot. If this is the case, unless the pony's access to rich grazing is restricted, he could become a cripple. In winter, grazing is generally poor which means that extra food should be provided.

In addition to the type of grass in the field it is essential to look at what else grows there. Some plants and trees are poisonous to ponies and if food is in short supply they may be tempted by harmful vegetation they would normally avoid.

- Is there a source of clean water? A pony will suffer from lack of water more quickly than lack of food. If there is no natural source, then a trough must be

A manger will prevent a grass-kept pony upsetting his feed in the field.

provided to make a constant supply of fresh water available.

- Is there any shelter in the field? This may be natural features like thick hedges, trees, or purpose built open sheds. If there is no shelter the pony must be brought in when the weather is extremely hot or cold, or failing this in winter, extra food and possibly rugs will be necessary.

- How many and what other animals share the land? Ponies like company, preferably of their own kind, but if there are many horses or ponies on a grazing area the land will gradually become "stale". This means that it must be treated with chemicals and fertilizers, or rested.

Ponies are wasteful grazers and will not eat grass in areas where there are droppings. A field grazed by ponies will eventually get very patchy and though it looks as if there is plenty of grass between the bare spots it is not really edible. It is difficult to avoid this wastage unless sheep are allowed to graze the same land as they will crop all the "toilet areas".

The important thing to remember is that a pony turned out indefinitely in a field cannot be expected to feed himself adequately throughout the year.

A pony which lives out will need supplementary feeding if he is expected to work hard or if the weather is cold.

Feeding the Stabled Pony

Assuming that a stabled pony is unable to break out and raid the feed bins the owner has total control over his diet. In this situation it is especially important that the owner supplies correct quantities of all the necessary goodies.

So just what are these "necessary goodies"? These vary according to the pony because each pony has his own particular requirements. But there are some basic principles you can follow.

Listed below are some of the things which affect *what* and *how much* a pony needs to eat:

Size and weight: Larger ponies generally need more food. To estimate a pony's weight use the following table as a guide.

12hh	300lbs
12.2hh	400lbs
13hh	500lbs
13.2hh	600lbs
14hh	700bs
14.2hh	800lbs

Age: Foals and young ponies need more protein and calcium in order to grow and develop properly. Estimate how large the youngster will be when fully grown and feed accordingly.

Work load: Like a car, a pony needs fuel to run and the more mileage he does and the faster he goes the more he will need to eat. A pony doing no work at all needs to eat approximately 1.8% of his body weight per day. So a 13hh pony weighing 500lbs needs about 9lbs of food each day. A pony doing light work needs about 2% of his body weight each day and if he is working much harder he may eat up to 3% of his body weight.

Temperament: Some ponies are sluggish and need pepping up. Others can be very naughty or lively if fed energy-giving foods, like oats.

Time of year: In winter, fat and carbohydrate rations need to be increased to help keep up the body temperature. This applies to ponies kept in or out.

General conditions: If a pony is young, in foal, or in poor condition, it is all the more important that the diet should be correctly balanced to ensure proper growth or recovery.

Metabolic rate: In horsy terms, ponies can be good or bad "doers". Just as some people seem to be able to eat cream cakes and chocolate and still stay skinny whilst others put on weight all too easily, so ponies' metabolisms can vary between the two extremes.

Ponies need food to fulfill a number of different functions –

- to keep warm
- for growth and body building
- to keep healthy and in condition
- for energy to work and play
- to reproduce (in the case of brood mares)

They need to take some of all these essential ingredients:
Water – most of the body is made up of water
Protein – proteins are body-building units
Fats – for energy and heat
Fibre – to help digestion
Vitamins and minerals – essential for health

What foods can provide all these requirements?

Grass: Good pasture in the spring and summer usually contains everything a pony needs.

Hay: If good quality, hay should make up the bulk of a pony's ration. Unless a pony is working very hard, about 70% of his ration should be hay and the other 30% concentrates. If he is stabled and fed too little hay he may suffer from digestive disorders and boredom, leading to bad habits such as crib biting. Good hay should smell sweet be dry and not mouldy or dusty. If a pony coughs when fed then the hay should be dampened. Alternatively, there are a number of "hayage" products now on the market which can provide the ideal solution.

Bran: This is bulk food because it is very high in fibre and helps digestion. It can also be used as a mild laxative and for feeding to ponies when they are ill or out of action. However, it does not contain enough calcium for foals and young ponies and this deficiency needs to be balanced out by feeding sugar beet or a calcium supplement.

Oats: These are by no means suitable for all ponies. They can be just the right thing for lethargic ponies but can make others giddy and so should be fed with caution.

Barley: It is not as energizing as oats but is often very suitable for keeping a pony warm in winter and for putting on weight. It should be fed ready cooked and flaked or crushed or boiled.

Flaked Maize: This provides a good source of energy but is no good for body building. Ponies usually like the taste.

Sugar Beet Pulp: When freshly prepared this is very tasty and moist. It is high in energy and calcium but not protein. The important thing to remember is that sugar beet pulp or nuts *must* be soaked in twice the volume of water for 24 hours. If fed dry it will expand as it absorbs moisture inside the body and can kill.

Milk Pellets: As these are high in protein they are particularly good for youngsters and for building up ponies which are in poor condition.

Ready Made Meals: There is a wide variety of cubes and coarse mixes which can take the headache out of feeding. They provide the correct proportions of all the essential ingredients. All you have to do is choose the best formula for the pony in question. The feed merchant or your vet should be able to offer advice.

A bran mash should be left to cool before being given to your pony.

Supplements: If a pony is fed on a traditional diet of hay and cereals and does not have access to good grazing he may need extra vitamins and minerals. During the winter, especially if a pony is constantly stabled, it is advisable to feed a broad spectrum vitamin/mineral supplement. A salt lick is also a good safeguard against deficiency as the pony can help himself when he needs it. (It is essential that ponies in hard work are fed salt or have access to a lick.)

Water: Should always be "on tap". If a pony has constant access to clean water then you do not need to worry whether he should be drinking before or after feeding and exercise. He will regulate this himself.

WINTER MENUS

For the 12.2hh pony living out and doing light work

Breakfast
1½ kilos (3lbs) hay
500 g (1lb) nuts or coarse mix

Evening Meal
1½ kilos (3lbs) hay
250 g (½lb) barley
250 g (½lb) sugar beet
250 g (½lb) bran

13hh pony stabled at night and out during the day and doing light work

Breakfast
1½ kilos (3lbs) hay
750 g (1½lbs) nuts

Evening Meal
2 kilos (4lbs) hay
250 g (½lb) barley or nuts
250 g (½lb) bran
250 g (½lb) sugar beet

13.2hh pony living out and not working

Breakfast
2 kilos (4lbs) hay
250 g (½lb) barley
250 g (½lb) bran

Evening Meal
2½ kilos (5lbs) hay
250 g (½lb) flaked maize
250 g (½lb) bran
250 g (½lb) sugar beet

14.2hh pony permanently stabled and doing fairly hard work

Breakfast
1½ kilos (3lbs) hay
750 g (1½lbs) oats
250 g (½lb) bran
250 g (½lb) sugar beet

Evening Meal
2 kilos (4lbs) hay
750 g (1½lbs) oats
250 g (½lb) bran
250 g (½lb) carrots

Lunch
1 kilos (2lbs) hay
1 kilo (2lbs) nuts or coarse mix

SUMMER MENUS

13.2hh jumping pony exercised daily, competing at weekends turned out for 5–6 hours grazing per day

Breakfast
500 g (1lb) nuts or coarse mix

Evening meal
1½ kilos (3lbs) hay
500 g (1lb) oats
250 g (½lb) bran

12.2hh gymkhana pony living out, exercised regularly and competing weekends

Weekdays:

Evening meal only
500 g (1lb) nuts *or*
375 g (¾lb) oats
125 g (¼lb) bran

Weekends:
Breakfast
500 g (1lb) nuts or oats

Evening meal
500 g (1lb) nuts or oats plus bran

Lunch
1 kilo (2lbs) hay

14hh show pony stabled and competing regularly

Breakfast
750 g (1½lbs) nuts
250 g (½lb) carrots

Evening meal
2 kilos (4lbs) hay
500 g (1lb) barley
250 g (½lb) bran
250 g (½lb) boiled linseed

Lunch
2 hours grazing

Treats

Bran Mash   1–1½ kilos (2–3lbs) bran
                  boiling water
                  salt
                  molasses or treacle (optional)

Pour boiling water over the bran in a feed bucket, add one tablespoonful salt and treacle if used and stir with a stick or wooden spoon until all the bran is dampened. Cover the bucket and leave it to cool. When the mixture is sufficiently cool feed immediately. Bran mashes are very easy to digest and are particularly good for ill or tired ponies.

Fruit and vegetable salad Slice carrots, apples, parsnips and a swede into strips. Mix in a base of dry bran and bind together with a little molasses. It is good to feed succulent food to ponies which don't have access to grass.

Guinness and Egg Pie

         250 g (½lb) crushed barley or oats
         250 g (½lb) bran
         bottle of Guinness or stout
         2 raw eggs

Mix the barley/oats and bran in a feed bucket. Add eggs, pour over stout and mix thoroughly. This dish is loaded with vitamins and protein and should not be fed too often!

Fruit and vegetable salad. Ideally the carrots should have been sliced in strips.

The Dos and Don'ts of Feeding

- Remember that a pony has only a small stomach and his daily ration should be split into two or if possible three feeds.

- Stick to a routine and feed at the same times each day.

- Do not exercise immediately after feeding, wait for at least an hour for the pony to digest his food.

- A pony's diet should be under constant review but avoid sudden changes as the digestive system will be unable to cope.

- Teeth should be checked regularly and rasped by the vet as sharp edges can cause discomfort when the pony eats. If a pony appears to be having difficulty in chewing or swallowing it is a good idea to examine his teeth.

- A pony should be wormed every 6–8 weeks throughout the year. It is a false economy not to worm a pony as the parasites will thrive on all the expensive food which is intended for the pony.

- Do not feed dusty or mouldy food. Cereals, nuts and even hay will all go off if kept too long. Arrange to share an order with friends if you get discounts on purchases. It is well worth while buying feed bins (or dustbins) to store foods as rats can very easily chew through sacks. Hay must also be kept dry and preferably in a ventilated place.

Feeding should be taken seriously. It is not always easy to hit on just the right formula for a particular pony and if problems occur with health, general condition or performance, vets or feed manufacturers should be able to offer useful advice. Correct feeding can make the difference between sickness and health and winning or losing so it is worth getting it right.

Sugar beet should be soaked before feeding.

HANDY HINTS

Rubber or metal dustbins make excellent feed containers. They are rat and mouseproof and cheaper than conventional bins.

● ● ●

When feeding a pony a titbit, place it on the flat of your palm with your fingers together so that he won't nibble you by accident. Carrots should be sliced lengthways as chunks could get stuck in his throat.

The Golden

The Pathan lay in the lush grass gazing across at the herd. The air was heavy with heat, somnolent bees droned amongst the thick hollyhocks and mulberry trees that hid him, and the light through the flowers threw exotic greens and pinks on to his loose white shirt-sleeves. The scent of the fallen fruit drifted headily to his nostrils. The afternoon held the silence of the mountains but in the young man's head there echoed the sounds of the *buz-kashi* – the wild thudding of unshod hooves, the harsh, excited cries of the tribesmen, the clash of metal as stirrup struck stirrup, the frenzy as the body of the goat – the spoil of the contest – was torn from the opponents' hands – and all around the heat and flies, the pungency of sweating horses and the rasping, choking dust of the plains.

The Pathan's family had played this sport since Alexander the Great had brought his armies out of Persia and in those days it had been an enemy who was thrown from rider to rider in the game. Now he had come deep into the mountains to search for a mount that would complement his skills and here, in this high valley, he had found what he desired.

Concealed at the edge of the grass he was looking out at a small group of mares and their young placidly cropping the turf of a natural meadow. Set between sheer grey outcrops of granite and starred with buttercups it spread around the multitude of streams that ran down the rock, watering this fertile pocket with melted snows. It was not unusual to come across a wild herd such as this, but there was one colt with them that had made the three-day journey worthwhile.

He was standing apart from the others drinking from a rivulet, not deeply as he would in the lowlands but in short, sucking gulps because of the iciness of the water, raising his head between mouthfuls and wrinkling back his lips. The Pathan could see that he was a yearling, old enough to have been displaced by his mother's last foal but too young to have been driven away by the stallion. There was mixed blood in the herd but in this one colt the strain of the Akhal-teke had risen and produced a wild horse as noble in line as any of the pure breed. Delicate and strong in conformation, he had the long neck and straight, elegant head of the Persian and he alone was that most precious colour – pale, glowing gold with black stockings on his clean, supple legs.

"The Golden", the young man whispered as he watched his prize move slowly from the water and brush his muzzle over the turf. Droplets still fell from the colt's chin and to free himself from them he splayed his hooves and shook himself vigorously to be rid of the chill of the stream, the tremor running from his ears to the stretch of his fine, dark tail, the spray glinting in the noon sun.

"The Golden", said the man softly and hungered for the colt with his madder-stained eyes.

He had been working in the *aylaq*, the summer pastures, when he had been told of the herd. Every year when the warm weather came, the men of his tribe left the

women to tend the crops in the valley and took the fat-tailed sheep, the goats and the black-and-white hump-backed cattle up into the high meadows to feed. Here they made butter and curds from the milk of their animals, storing it in the rivers until it was needed, and carried it down the mountainside on their backs to trade in the markets.

On that evening three days ago he had been squatting beside his fire boiling curds to pack into a goat-skin, when a caravan of Kafirs had wound down the pass driving a herd of loose horses before them. They had set their tents beside the Pathan's stone hut and as the night-winds gathered and the stars froze in the darkness of the moonless sky, the nomads drew about his fire and told him of the wild horses of the remote hills. For centuries Arabs, Turkmene and Akhaltekes had been released there to run with the native ponies and even now it was possible to find such a one unclaimed; they themselves had seen a colt worthy of a prince and would have caught him to sell in Kabul if luck had been with them. They had come upon the herd he saw here tethered beside their tents, and had captured the stallion with most of the mares and young. But a handful of mares had escaped – and with them had been a golden colt as perfect as the sun in heaven.

The Pathan had waited for the nomads to make their way down the hillside in the early morning and then left his work in the fields. He had known when he heard them talk that this would be the horse that would carry him proudly into the *buz-kashi*. He packed dried apricots and thin, fried wheatbread into his carrying-skin for the journey and barley rolled into balls with sheep-fat for the colt. Tying a halter about his waist

92

he retraced the Kafirs' route over the pass and came deep into the lonely country beyond. For two nights he had slept wrapped in his sheepskin under the sky and now he was content to lie in the heat of midday and admire the treasure before him.

As the afternoon faded and the cool of the evening was felt in the air the colt wandered nearer his watcher and the young man knew that his chance had come. Stealthily he rose to his feet and left his hiding-place to stand revealed between the colt and the mares. Even he, who was so used to animals, had not expected such suspicion. At once all heads were lifted, all ears pricked. The golden colt backed two uncertain paces from the stranger, then broke into a leggy canter and tried to bolt past the Pathan to the safety of his mother. Running to prevent the colt's escape the man clapped his hands and cried out to scatter the mares. In

her agitation, the colt's mother thought only of protecting her youngest foal and followed the herd as they galloped headlong through the narrow entrance to the valley, leaving her colt to his own defences.

Nostrils flared, the colt dodged and kicked to be free of his pursuer, rearing into sharp turns that cut the turf beneath his hooves and splashing through the stream. But the Pathan had grown up in the hills cornering runaways from the milk-herds and he could not be thrown off by such an inexperienced young horse. Instead of tiring he laughed as he ran, delighting in the agility of the colt which would serve him so well in the game.

At last the colt sensed that he must abandon the mares, and racing towards the rocks he fled into a ravine that led upwards from the valley floor. Here the grass ended and the path became a jumble of dust and fallen

93

stones, dangerous to the pounding feet of the colt as he climbed steeply towards the mountaintop. The Pathan now climbed more slowly in the wake of his prize, so that the colt would slacken speed thinking he was no longer followed: dearly as he wanted this horse he would rather risk losing him than let him hurt himself in his flight.

They climbed for two hours; the colt steadily and more calmly, the man never falling so far behind that he could not hear the grate and stamp of hooves on loose granite. The gorge was bare and desolate; they had left the tree-line far beneath them and no bush or grass clung to the rock-walls, no sound reached them but their own steps and the clatter of the ibex nearby. The rocks stood out in relief as the sun went down and darkness was falling as they squeezed through the tapering entrance to the ravine into the circle of sheer rock that formed its beginning. The Pathan stood in ·the gap and watched the colt search fruitlessly for an escape, then turn and face his captor. The young man squatted amongst the boulders and waited for there to be enough light to win The Golden's trust.

All night he talked softly to the horse until the snows above them showed violet and grey in the dawn. Then, taking his goat-skin, he poured water into the hollow of a rock and after the colt had drunk laid out the barley and sweet, soft apples of his village for him to eat. The colt sniffed the food and looked up at the young man as if undecided. Then, seeing only kindness, he took an apple delicately into his mouth. And as he ate the Pathan rested a hand gently on the golden neck and smiled.

Understanding Ponies

Ponies, like any animals can have very different personalities. Some are quiet and reliable, others sensitive or hot-headed. However, one thing they all have in common is a rather nervous mentality. For millions of years during their development, ponies, as grass eaters, were prey for the carnivores like lions, tigers and wolves. They learnt to be constantly on the look-out for danger in the bushes and developed the instinct to run first and think later. A sudden movement spotted out of the corner of the eye could be a lion looking for lunch so the safest course of action was – and still is – to run off at once. This instinct has become so deeply ingrained that even now, after thousands of years of domestication, ponies are still basically alert and easily startled animals.

Once you understand this you'll see why ponies sometimes behave in the mystifying way they do: shying at paper bags, or jumping when you come into the stable unexpectedly. You'll learn to treat them with consideration and confidence, to reassure them and to avoid upsetting them.

However, to be able really to get on with ponies you need to understand a bit more about what they are trying to say. It is not enough to know that a pony can be easily startled, you need to be able to recognize the signs that something is upsetting or alerting him!

When we train a pony we teach him to understand what the rider wants him to do. He learns that pressure from the rider's legs means go faster, pressure on one rein means move to that side and on both reins, slow down or stop.

But how can we tell what a pony is trying to say to *us*? Whether they are happy, nervous or in pain? Unlike humans, ponies don't try to hide their feelings, so once you know the signs to watch out for, it can be quite easy to understand what is going on inside their heads.

Ponies communicate amongst themselves by means of signs and facial expressions. Let's start with the face of a healthy, happy pony. He will have a calm, alert

One ear flicked back to listen to the rider

Bandy objects to having his girth tightened.

expression with his ears pricked towards whatever attracts his attention; a titbit in your hand maybe, or his best friend passing by. His eyes will be soft with an enquiring look which shows he is interested in everything that is going on around him.

A pony's ears are an important clue to what he is thinking. They usually point towards whatever is holding his attention, whether it is you with his feed or a frightening lorry or piece of paper in the road. If, whilst you are riding, one or both ears flick back towards you, this is because he is paying attention to the aids you are giving him. In the same way, if he senses something he doesn't like coming up behind him, such as a heavy lorry, or a barking dog, his ears will go back again to assess the danger.

When you are jumping, your pony's ears should be pricked towards the approaching fence to show he is taking an interest in it and intending to jump. If his ears are not aiming in the direction you are going you can be pretty sure he is not paying attention and is quite likely to refuse or knock the jump down when he actually reaches it.

Sometimes, however, he can have his ears pricked firmly towards a jump while thinking that, just like the paper bag in the road, although it is not immediately frightening, he is unsure of it and might well refuse or shy away. In this case, you will be able to sense his uncertainty by the way he approaches the fence. His tail may be swishing behind you, which is a sure sign of anger or distress and he will be going forward reluctantly, almost as if he is "back pedalling".

A pony can also put his ears back as a sign of aggression and warning. In this case the action will be accompanied by wrinkled nostrils, a swishing tail and a generally cross expression and if a pony approaches you like this you can be pretty certain he means to bite!

However sometimes a pony will put his ears back simply as a sign of honest effort. Watch a racehorse galloping flat out – his ears will be back and he'll have a determined expression which shows that he is trying as hard as he can.

Another very expressive part of your pony's body is his tail. If he carries it gaily it is a sign that he is quite happy. If he clamps it between his hindlegs it is a sign that he is worried about something behind him.

If the latter is the case it might be closely followed by another easily recognized pony signal, the one that tells you he is about to kick. A pony who is about to lash out will lift his tail, flick his ears back to aim and, of course, lift a hindleg. Watch out!

Similarly, if a pony is about to buck, you will see or feel him swish his tail as he humps his back and drops his head with his ears back. Once you recognize the signals you will be able to take evasive action by getting his head up with the reins and riding him on strongly.

Whilst on the subject of feet, you will often see a pony rest a hindleg when he is bored or relaxed and contented. A resting foreleg, though, is a sign of pain and you should check the foot for heat or injury.

Stamping a foot can be a sign of irritation either with a person, another pony or simply with flies buzzing around the legs. Some ponies stamp, swish and nip when you are tightening their girths, probably because someone has hurt them by girthing up too tightly or too quickly in the past. Although it may just be a habit it can also be a sign that the skin under the girth is being pinched, so take it as a warning that you should girth up gently and smooth down the skin with your hand.

You'll sometimes see a pony curl its top lip up and back, showing its teeth and pointing its nose to the sky. It will look as if it's laughing but it's not. This is a sign of nausea, and the pony will have smelt or tasted something unpleasant. I once visited a friend's stables where I was given some cheese and onion sandwiches for lunch. When I went out to see the horses every one I touched turned its lips up as soon as it smelled my hands! I had forgotten about the onions and felt most hurt!

Yuk! Onions!

Your pony's behaviour will soon tell you whether he is well and happy or sick and in pain. Take a pony who is standing in a field, a little away from the others, with his head down, and ears relaxed. He may be just resting or he may be ill: the only way you can tell is by approaching him. If he greets you listlessly suspect illness, if he perks up and looks for a titbit or moves away in case you are trying to catch him, then he was probably only dozing or bored. You will soon learn to "feel" the difference and recognize the symptoms if a pony is really ill.

Colic, a tummy ache, is a fairly common complaint and the pony will stamp its feet, bite its flanks, swish its tail and generally appear worried or frightened. Patchy sweating indicates pain and the pony might want to get down to roll. If you see all these signs, call your vet at once.

Ponies often roll for fun but to tell if he is happy or in pain, watch him closely afterwards. If he gets up and has a good shake then you know he's all right. If he doesn't shake, he could be unwell so watch him closely for other symptoms.

A pony's voice, like a human's, can range from very low and gentle to high, loud and screaming. If you go to his box first thing in the morning, he will probably give you a low nicker of welcome. If you offer him a titbit, it will sound more animated, and if you come along with a bucket containing his breakfast it could range from a louder nicker, with excitement, to an outright neigh. This will be accompanied by pricked ears and quivering nostrils to show he is pleased to see you.

Ponies often neigh or whinney to their friends in the distance and when they are free together in a field and having a little skirmish, you will hear all sorts of squeals of warning, protest or delight.

You can learn a great deal by studying pony behaviour and as you get to know ponies better you will find that they really have quite a lot to say to us. Once you come to understand ponies' body language you will find that you get more and more fun from your associations with them.

Your Pony and the Vet

On the whole, ponies are much hardier animals than horses and need less veterinary attention. However, this doesn't mean that they are always 100% healthy so pony owners should still keep a weather eye open for tell-tale signs of ill health. Listlessness, a staring coat, coughing and loss of appetite are all signs that something is amiss and should be a signal to call out your vet.

In the winter it is especially important to examine a pony's skin and limbs properly, particularly if he is turned out. Their thick coats can often disguise thinness or injuries.

Many problems can be forestalled by routine preventative treatment, and if you think of it as a kind of insurance, you will realize it is worth every penny. Tetanus and influenza vaccines should be renewed annually, as tetanus in particular, a serious disease which can be contracted through the smallest scratch, can kill. Ponies should also be wormed every six to eight weeks to prevent infestation and their teeth should be checked annually. Your vet will advise you on all these matters and many vets issue individual record cards so that you can make sure your pony's worming doses and vaccinations are always kept up to date.

If your pony is fed and cared for properly he should stay fit and happy for most of the time. However, ponies like any other animal, suffer from diseases and there are a number to which they seem particularly prone.

Laminitis

This is an inflammation of the laminae inside the hoof and causes acute pain and lameness. It often seems to be triggered by

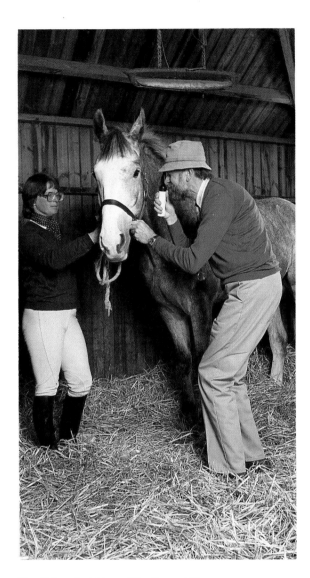

Don't be afraid to call in the vet if you're worried.

over-eating, particularly lush, spring grass, and overweight ponies are especially prone. Affected ponies are very reluctant to move and will stand with the weight on their heels, and the toes of their feet pointing slightly upwards to try and relieve the pain.

Resting the weight on the heels is a telltale sign of laminitis.

The feet can get so hot that they will steam if water is splashed on them.

A vet will treat laminitis with painkillers and anti-inflammatory drugs but unfortunately once a pony has had an attack its feet will generally suffer some long-term damage and in very severe cases the pony may have to be destroyed. Prevention is far better than cure and pony owners should be very careful to restrict lush grazing, especially in the spring.

Sweet Itch

A second ailment almost exclusively restricted to ponies is sweet itch. This is an itchy condition of the skin, generally found in the summer, which is probably caused by oversensitivity to the bites of certain species of midge. Unless the pony can be stopped rubbing and scratching it can make a terrible mess of its mane and tail. Again prevention is better than cure and ponies which suffer from the condition should be stabled at dusk and dawn when the midges are biting. A vet can prescribe antiseptics and antibiotics to treat sweet itch and insect repellents can help to keep the midges away. In winter when there are no midges, the pony's damaged mane and tail will usually grow again.

Worms

As many ponies live out at grass for long periods of time, they are very likely to pick up worm infestation. This is by far the most important medical condition to affect ponies and unfortunately accounts for many deaths each year. Ponies harbour various types of worm but the most significant are the redworms which lay thousands of eggs a day, infesting pasture and hence carrying on the life-cycle. They live in the pony's intestines but migrate through the body, causing even more damage as they go. If a pony is affected by worms it will usually lose weight and become anaemic and may suffer bouts of colic and diarrhoea. Fortunately modern medicines can deal with worms very efficiently and routine worming will prevent any of this occurring.

Colic

Colic, an acute pain in the abdomen, is a particularly distressing condition and it is important to be able to recognize the symptoms so that help can be summoned quickly. A pony with colic will look miserable, pawing the ground with its front feet, turning and looking at its flanks anxiously, swishing its tail, sweating, trembling, breathing rapidly, rolling violently or kicking its flanks. There are various causes of colic ranging from digestive upsets, worm infestations and sometimes catastrophes like twisted intestines. Cases should never be ignored in the hope that they will right themselves; a vet will be able to give a painkiller and diagnose the cause so it can be treated at source.

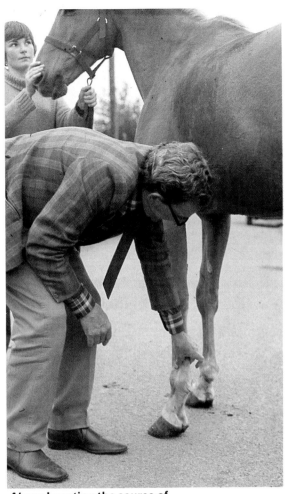

Above Locating the source of lameness.
Below Teeth should be checked regularly.

HANDY HINT

If a pony is injured and bleeding quite badly, wrap a hard object like a stone in a piece of clean material and press it hard on the wound or the blood vessel just above it. Call the vet right away.

Strangles

Strangles is a respiratory condition, which is similar to tonsillitis. Ponies get sore throats the same way as you do and are likely to have a high temperature and fever, a thick yellowish nasal discharge, slight cough and swollen glands in the throat which can form abcesses and burst. Fortunately strangles is easily treated with antibiotics, but it is highly contagious and can spread rapidly through a stable yard. To avoid this happening, any pony with a nasal discharge and a temperature should be isolated and the vet called immediately.

Coughing

Coughing is really a symptom, not a disease in its own right, but it is used as a convenient blanket term to cover all sorts of virus infections. Probably the best known virus to cause coughing is influenza, and as it is highly infectious it is well worth vaccinating a pony against it.

Most of the viruses show similar symptoms, a mild fever, a few days off colour and coughing. There may be a nasal discharge, but this is usually very slight and nothing compared to the amount seen in strangles. Unfortunately, there is no specific treatment for virus infections, although drugs and medicines can help to make the pony feel better, and will prevent any complicating infections occurring at the same time. The virus will burn itself out and the pony return to work in about three or four weeks. Again, affected ponies should be isolated if possible.

Wounds

Pony injuries should be treated in much the same way as human ones, remembering that a horse's skin is more liable to contamination than ours, especially the lower limbs which are often covered in mud! As the skin of the lower limbs is very tight and it is difficult to immobilize a pony, wounds in these regions are potentially dangerous. They are slow to heal and there is often a vital structure, such as a joint or tendon, very close to the skin. It is always best to seek expert advice when treating wounds, and sometimes just a phone call to your vet can be enough. If the pony is not protected against tetanus it will need a vaccination immediately.

An example of a particularly easily contaminated wound is a puncture to the sole of the foot. This can be caused by treading on a flint, piece of glass or other sharp object and will cause a lot of pain and lameness. Puncture wounds are usually treated by opening up the area. This allows infected material to drain and makes it easier to apply drugs. Bandages and special boots can be used to cover the foot so the wound can heal in a clean environment.

Bleeding from a wound can generally be controlled by applying pressure with a wad of gamgee. Tourniquets are unnecessary and as they can be extremely dangerous, should never be used as a first aid measure. Your vet may decide to stitch the wound to help it heal. Either way he will clean it with antiseptic and will probably apply an antiseptic or antibiotic dressing. If the injury cannot be bandaged a wound powder can be puffed on.

The wound will need re-dressing every day for the first week – your vet will show you how. Look for signs of infection; yellowish pus over the wound, swelling, pain or lameness and if these occur call the vet again.

A serious wound requires the vet's attention. He will decide whether it needs stitching, and will make sure it is cleaned thoroughly before applying a dressing.

Cracked Heels

This is common in ponies who are turned out in the winter and is caused by the skin in the heel region becoming chapped and dirty. The area may be inflamed and swollen and in bad cases the pony could even be lame. Your vet will prescribe antibiotics to treat the condition and you must try to keep the pony's heels as clean and dry as possible. Barrier cream applied to the heels before you turn the pony out each day can help prevent cracked heels.

Girth Galls

Galls are usually caused by pressure or friction from an ill-fitting saddle or girth. This can cause inflammation or bleeding particularly behind your pony's elbows or on the withers. The obvious treatment is to stop using the offending tack until the gall is healed and antibiotics may be necessary if the area has become infected. To make sure it doesn't happen again, ask your saddler to check the fit of your tack and always clean it after every ride so that the leather stays soft and supple.

The Pony Owner's First Aid Kit

If your pony is ill or injured you should call the vet. He will advise on treatment and the following items may be useful when you come to carry out his instructions.

Bandages   Woollen stable bandages to keep a sick pony warm
Stretchy tail bandages to support a strained leg

Cotton wool   For applying dressing

Gamgee   To dress wounds

Tulle   A non-adherent dressing

Antiseptic solution   Diluted to bathe wounds

Antiseptic Cream/Powder

Thermometer   Only to be used if someone knows how to use it properly

Scissors   To be kept only for use in the first aid kit

Colic drenches or cough medicines are not really necessary as they are generally ineffective and no substitute for professional help.

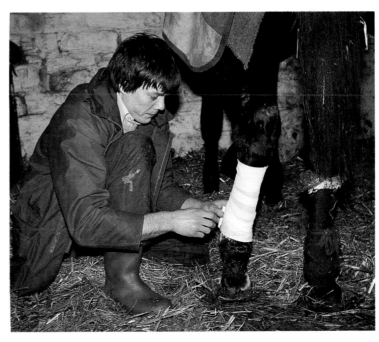

Building Your Own Jumps

A full set of jumps is beyond most people's budget but that doesn't mean you need resort to the other extreme: a few rusty oil drums, a hotch potch of broken poles, three upturned buckets supporting a slender sapling and two distinctly wobbly cavalletti!

If this inventory sounds embarrassingly familiar then isn't it time you did something about your jumping equipment? The sort of obstacles I've described are flimsy and uninviting and do nothing to improve your pony's jumping ability or style. After all, they're not the sort of thing he's likely to meet at your local show. A paddock littered with such debris is unsightly and can be dangerous, as your pony could easily injure himself on some of your "jumps".

It is possible to acquire cheaply the sort of things which can be converted into jumps. But most importantly, your jumps must be safe. They must have no sharp or protruding edges and their supports must be stabilized. They must be solid and inviting-looking with enough poles or fillers. You need a variety of shapes – uprights, spreads, hog's backs, parallels – and each obstacle must be as versatile as possible. A horse or pony judges where to take off by looking at the base of the jump, so make sure you have adequate ground lines. And remember, apart from a hog's back, the highest pole in a jump must be at the back. Fences which are to be tackled from both directions must have a ground line on both sides and the highest point must still be the farthest away point so that only uprights, parallels and hog's backs fit the bill here.

Set out to acquire six jumps, four of which can be jumped both ways, which will give you a course of ten fences. Ideally these should include one permanent, four mobile and one temporary obstacle.

Permanent jumps are usually cross-country type fences, such as ditches, banks or log piles. They encourage careful jumping and provide a bit of variety from the usual coloured poles.

Mobile jumps allow you to be versatile. As well as conventional wings, poles and fillers, these can include tyres and barrels.

A temporary obstacle is one made of materials which cannot be left in the field. This can be straw bales, brush or other greenery which make safe jumps but will deteriorate in bad weather.

All the materials listed below are ones that can be acquired reasonably easily and cheaply – sometimes even for nothing!

Logs

Probably the easiest permanent jump to construct is a log pile. See if you can get a load of logs from a local supplier. Decide on

a level place in your paddock which allows the jump to be approached from several angles and clear away the grass, stones and weeds. Pick out regular shaped logs and lay out a complete outline of the shape of your jump between nine and fifteen feet long with two or three differing heights and widths.

Once the "pattern" of your log pile is laid out on the ground, add layer after layer of wood, fitting the logs tightly together like doing a jigsaw puzzle! As your pile gets higher make it gradually narrower. Be sure that the logs which you put on the top layer have no sharp protruding bits on them.

Your finished product will be a solid, long lasting and inviting jump.

Oil Drums

Probably the most versatile item for mobile jumps is the familiar oil drum. Ask around and acquire as many of these as possible; wash and scrub them out thoroughly, then go over them with sandpaper when they are dry. You can paint the drums – all one colour or in contrasting colours – but be sure that you use lead-free paint; especially if the jumps are to be in the field where your pony grazes, as lead-based paints are extremely poisonous.

When setting up your jumps use small wooden wedges to keep the barrels in place – stones would do, but wedges are much better.

Here are some suggestions for using your oil drums:

These basic oil drum jumps can be made more difficult by the addition of poles painted in matching or contrasting colours:

As you can see, drums are also invaluable as wings and supports. They can be used with other oil drums or with poles, tyres and other fillers.

105

Brush Fences

There are various methods of building brush fences. You can have wooden containers specially made to hold your greenery but a cheaper alternative is to try and beg some old plastic milk crates from your local dairy. Don't take any broken ones with sharp edges though. You will need six for your jump and four for your wings. Place a large stone in the bottom of each for stability then fill with your brush or twigs. The spaces for the milk bottles make ideal "holders". You can make the brush more firm by "bunching" it into bundles with string or elastic bands before firmly packing it into the base. The height of the jump will be dictated by the length of the brush you cut. Wooden fruit boxes may be used in place of milk crates following the same procedure.

Poles

It's impossible to have a versatile, realistic course without at least some jumping poles and money sensibly spent here is very well spent indeed. Go to a reputable timber yard and ask for straight poles, well dried and with their bark removed, of at least nine feet in length (preferably ten to twelve feet). They should be at least four inches in diameter, five to six inches for preference. If you have ten poles, you could keep three rustic, paint two in plain white and five in coloured stripes.

When not in use, keep poles off the ground or they will rot very quickly. Half tyres nailed to fence posts at appropriate distances apart serve as good pole holders.

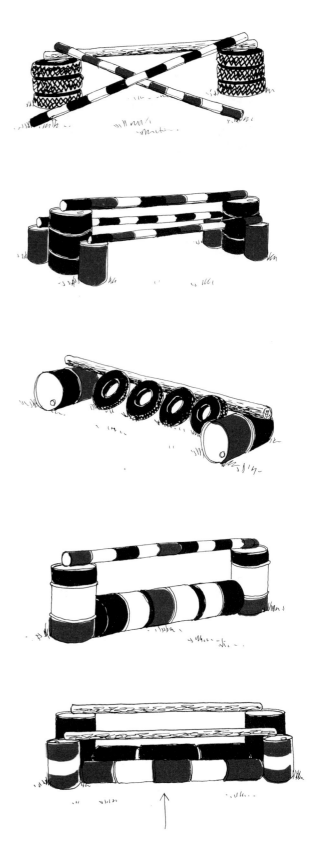

Some alternative ways of combining barrels, tyres and poles. The arrows indicate the direction in which the jump should be approached.

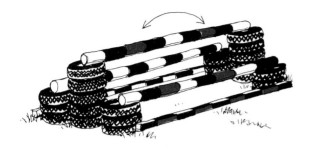

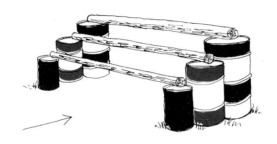

Fillers

Fillers can be made from odds and ends such as wooden doors and gates. They must have no protruding nails or edges and they must be free standing. You might be able to get a damaged wooden gate quite cheaply from a local farmer, and if you lean it against barrels or wings it won't fall if you hit it. Remove the hinges and the broken top spar and saw the outside supports flush with the next spar. Reinforce broken lower spars with wood strappings, wire-brush the wood, then treat it with creosote or preservatives or paint it white. Finally, metal supports need to be screwed at either end. A door may be given the same treatment.

Another very adaptable item for jumps is a supply of used car tyres. Like barrels, they can be used as wings or as fillers.

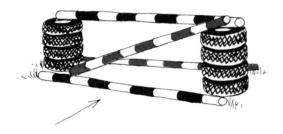

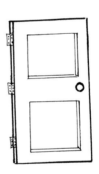

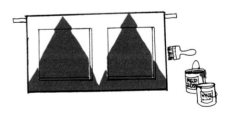

When building jumps make sure that the highest pole is always at the back, as a lower pole could be obscured and could cause your pony to fall.

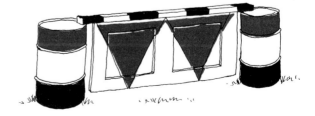

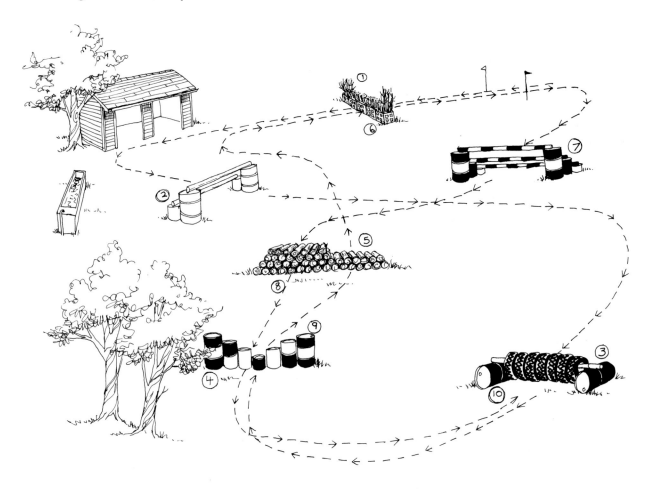

With a little planning, you need only half a dozen home-made jumps to be able to build a variety of interesting courses.

Bags and Bales (Temporary Jumps)
You can also utilize polythene fertilizer bags and feed sacks. Paper feed sacks can be filled with crumpled newspaper with a few stones to weight them and then stacked to make a challenging cross country fence. The polythene variety can be securely stapled to two poles or the bags can be slit at the sides and the poles passed through them.

Straw bales can also be used to make a temporary fence. Lay out five bales on their sides with three in the middle and two at each end as wings. Then, carefully lay your greenery along the bales, poking the long pieces through the strings to keep it in place and criss crossing shorter pieces along the base.

Here is a possible course, using just the sort of home-made jumps I have been talking about. There are almost endless other possibilities if you put your mind to it!

Lots of ideas to be going on with, so happy do-it-yourself jump making!

HANDY HINT
When planning a jumping course, site your first fence so that you jump towards rather than away from the field gate or stables. This will encourage your pony to jump freely and start the course on a good note.

Riding Holidays

Imagine waking up one summer's morning, rushing outside with a crowd of friends, tacking up your ponies and setting off for the day across some of the most beautiful countryside in Britain. If you go on a riding holiday that's just what you can expect to do.

Holidays like these are tailor made for people without ponies. No need to worry about how well you can ride as there'll be experienced instructors to keep an eye on you and make sure you are allocated a pony you can handle. A few basic lessons will put you on the right track and then you'll be able to set out across the sort of countryside that most pony owners would give their eye teeth for: rolling moorland, shady woods, logs and ditches to jump. At the end of the day there'll be barbecues, discos, quizzes or cinema trips with swimming, shopping expeditions and gymkhanas fitted into the timetable as well.

A riding holiday is a good way to find out whether you really would like a pony of your own. Most centres will let you "adopt" a pony for your stay, feeding and grooming as well as riding it, and you'll learn how to handle ponies, catch them, turn them out, tack them up – in fact all the things most riding schools don't have time to teach their clients.

If you're bitten by the riding holiday bug you'll want to go back again year in, year out, but it is important to find a good centre. Otherwise you could be in for a big disappointment. Nothing is worse than setting out for the day on a thin, tired pony which you are sure would have been happier staying at home.

On the first day of her holiday Emma is allocated a pony.

So where do you start to look? Magazines like PONY carry lots of advertisements for holiday centres, particularly at the beginning of the year. Decide which area you prefer, probably not too far from home, and look for a centre which is approved by the British Horse Society or the Ponies of Britain. Then write for a selection of brochures and take your pick!

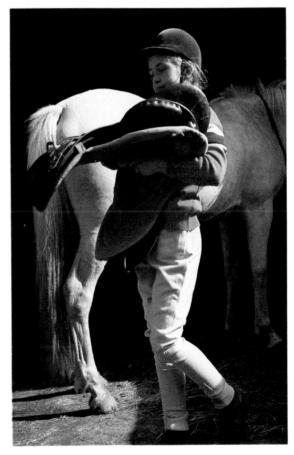

Left Breakfast time at a Riding Centre in Somerset and the riders plan their day. Emma's holiday included day rides across the Quantock hills, a gallop on the beach, a trip round the cross-country course and shopping expeditions to the nearby town. Swimming, grass-sledging, videos, barbecues and discos meant the evenings were busy as well. Emma's verdict? "I'll definitely go again!"

Ideally it is best to be able to visit a centre before you book your holiday but if this isn't possible look at the photos in the brochures carefully. Do the ponies look clean and well fed? Are the riders all wearing hats? At least some of the staff should be BHS qualified and it is a bonus if the centre has some facilities for indoor riding – in case it rains!

For more information about approved holiday centres send a stamped addressed envelope to: The British Horse Society, British Equestrian Centre, Stoneleigh, Kenilworth, Warwickshire CV8 2LR. Ponies of Britain, Chesham House, 56 Green Road, Sawtry, Huntingdon.

Hat Trick

"Those who aren't jumping, go through the gap," said David, standing up in his stirrups, laying one calming hand on Midnight's gleaming neck, and looking back at the ride that trotted up the hill behind him.

Ignoring my friend Angie's hard stare boring into the back of my neck, I turned Sceptre towards the gap. I wasn't jumping. I didn't care what anyone said. Not even David.

David Benson owns the riding school where Angie and I ride. We think he is absolutely fantastic. He is about thirty years old, has black hair and blue eyes and we send him a Valentine every year. He rides in three-day events. Last year he was sixth at Badminton and he cannot understand how anyone could want to ride and not want to jump. Angie can't either.

"Kate!" exclaimed Angie, in a voice that sent every rabbit for miles around dashing for shelter. "You're jumping."

"No," I said.

"Kate," said David, alerted by Angie's foghorn bellow, "over the wall. None of this creeping through gaps."

"It's for your own good," said Angie. "You know what you're like when you don't jump. Sodden all week. Keep Sceptre in behind me. She'll jump all right if you let her follow Lady."

"I don't want to."

"Of course you do," said Angie.

"Keep behind me," said David as Midnight flew at the wall, soaring over it in a smooth arc.

And of course I did want to jump. Wanted and wanted to jump, if only I could

have jumped the way David did – soaring, almost flying – but it was never like that when I jumped.

Angie kicked Lady at the two foot high, dry-stone wall and Lady bucketed over. "Come on, come on," she yelled at me but I clung tightly on to Sceptre's reins, keeping her back until the four other riding school horses had all jumped.

"Get a move on, Kate," David commanded.

I turned Sceptre at the wall, still holding tightly on to her reins, and trotted her at the stone barricade which loomed in front of me higher than the wall at the White City. Clutching handfuls of mane I shut my eyes and Sceptre stopped. We repeated our performance three times.

"Oh well, take her through the gap," said David, who months and months ago, had given up all hope of teaching me to jump.

"It's Sceptre. She won't jump," I said, knowing perfectly well that it wasn't Sceptre's fault. It was mine. I had no intention of letting her jump. I dreaded those terrible moments when I felt my pony soar upwards leaving me behind; when I saw her neck stretching out in front of me and then the sickening jolt as I bashed down on the saddle at the other side of the jump. Or, worse still, saw the ground rush up to meet me as I crashed into it.

"You can jump Firebird. He'll jump for you," said Lydia, and she leapt off the chestnut pony she was riding and led him back through the gap.

Lydia Saunders is hated by Angie and me. She is always there, being better and knowing more than we do. If she were even to mention to her parents that she wanted a pony they would buy one for her. We know this because she has told us so herself, many times. Lydia prefers to come to the riding school. Angie says it is so she can show off, meaning her expensive riding clothes, her leather boots and, worst of all, her private riding lessons with David.

"Not likely," I cried, shocked at the very idea of even getting on Firebird, never mind jumping him.

"Don't tell me you're scared," sneered Lydia.

I hadn't been going to tell her, but was quite willing to agree that I was, when Angie's foghorn voice blasted any such notions out of my head.

"Of course she's not scared," roared Angie. "Are you, Kate? Of course you're not!"

Faced with Angie's certainty I felt the flesh tighten on my bones and my stomach sink. I was going to have to jump. It was about to happen.

When I dismounted I could hardly stand on my jelly legs.

Lydia snatched Sceptre's reins from me and held Firebird while I mounted. The chestnut pony was narrow between my knees after the Highland bulk of Sceptre; his arching neck was high in front of me. I gathered up my reins and instantly, with his head in the air, Firebird shot at the wall. I was only conscious of our speed. Tears blinded me. Then there were Angie's screams in my ears as Firebird jumped me out of the saddle and I went slamming into the ground.

"You should have known," said Angie as we walked home together. "There was bound to be something dodgy when Lydia Saunders suggested it."

"You knew all along, I suppose. Pity you didn't mention it. Actually if you hadn't shouted to begin with I could have gone through the gap and no one would have noticed."

My shoulder ached where it had hit the ground. My muddied jodhs and jacket meant that I would need to explain to my mother what had happened. She would not be pleased.

"You could have gone through the gap," echoed Angie scornfully. "Is that how you want to live? Going through gaps all your life?"

"It is," I said. "I am a gap person. I ask no more of life."

Angie snorted in disgust. "We shall see about that," she said. "I ask more of life than to spend my days being best friend to a gap."

It was Saturday afternoon when I had parted company with Firebird. Spectacularly. I knew it was a spectacular fall because next morning, when Angie and I were mucking out, David came round to ask me how I was. He only does that when he has been worried about bringing an ambulance over the moor to retrieve the fallen.

"I'll take your name out of the bucket," he said sarcastically, knowing very well that my name never went into the bucket.

Every Easter Miss Peel's riding school, about twenty miles away, holds a cross country competition for the pupils of the various riding schools in the county. Children who have their own ponies are banned. It is only for poor, ponyless waifs like ourselves. A week before the competition David writes the names of all the hopefuls on pieces of paper, puts them in a bucket and draws out the lucky five. My name never goes into the draw.

"You will leave Kate's name in the bucket," stated Angie. "This year she is competing."

"Winged pigs!" exclaimed David.

Before I had time to protest, David's father, who is a banker, shouted across the yard that David was wanted on the phone and David hurried into the house.

The draw took place in the tackroom that afternoon. The competition was next Saturday.

Lydia was drawn first to ride Firebird.

"Surprise, surprise," said Angie.

By the time David reached Bomber, the fifth and last pony, neither Angie nor I had had our names drawn from the bucket. Bomber had been David's first cross country pony. She was the best draw, unless you happened to be me.

"And to ride Bomber," announced David, pausing with the piece of paper in his hand.

"Please, please not me," I prayed silently.

"Kate."

Angie made a noise like a deflating balloon but it was drowned by Lydia's comment.

"And what's Kate going to do on Bomber? Sit and watch?" she exploded.

I hardly heard her. I was in deepest shock. Everyone else longing to draw Bomber and it had to be me. Once, and once only, I had ridden Bomber. She was built like a tank with a tree-trunk leg at each corner. Her Roman-nosed head was welded to the end of her short, muscled neck and her quarters would have propelled her over the moon. I could remember nothing of my ride on her except the pounding terror of being on a galloping horse who is totally out of control. Never would I be able to ride her over Miss Peel's cross country jumps.

"Don't be so daft," said Angie turning on

Lydia. Her own hopes dead, she beamed the searchlight of her energy directly at me. "Kate's riding her and what's more she's going to win."

All week I existed in an icy clutch of fear. I could think of nothing but being catapulted from the saddle by Bomber's kangaroo leaps, to go whamming into the ground. I heard the bones in my neck crunch, and the sharp crack of a broken arm or leg. I considered the possibilities of instant toothache, tonsillitis or 'flu but I knew that Angie was quite capable of dragging me from my sick bed.

"Angie, please, *you* ride her," I pleaded.

"Oh don't be so feeble. I tell you, you are going to win on Saturday. All you have to do is sit there and Bomber will take you round."

It wasn't until I was in bed on Friday night that my brainwave hit me. I would leave my hard hat at home. Miss Peel would never allow me to compete without a hat. If anyone offered to lend me a hat I would tell them that I had an infectious scalp disease.

"Got everything?" David asked. "There's no turning back."

It was Saturday morning and he was sitting at the wheel of his float ready to drive us all to Miss Peel's. Angie and I were in the cabin with him, the others were in the back of the float with our five mounts.

Angie's gimlet eye's sussed me out.

"Have you got your hat?" she said.

I nodded, blushing furiously.

"Where?" demanded Angie, knowing that when I lie I go scarlet in the face.

It took her only a few seconds to realize that I had no hat.

"Don't tell me!" shouted David. "Need to stop and unlock the tackroom. Bound to be one in there you can borrow."

"I can't borrow . . ." I began, but my burning cheeks gave me away.

"She could borrow yours," suggested Angie. "We know it fits because we tried it on one day."

"Did we indeed. Least that would save some time. We're late enough as it is. Nip out and get it. On the hallstand by the door."

"I know," Angie said and nipped.

"Got it," she announced climbing back into the cab. "Could only find your bowler."

"That ancient relic," said David, starting up the float, checking the road for traffic. "Mum must have routed it out from the attic. I wore that when I first started competing. Still, it'll do. Miss Peel won't be bothering about correct turn out."

When we had unboxed the ponies at Miss Peel's David told us to ride them in.

"Walk her round in circles," commanded Angie.

I did as I was told. Bomber was power packed beneath me. I had no control over her. Sick with terror, I did not know how I had ever been so crazy as to allow this to happen to me. But soon it would be over. I would have fallen off and that would be that.

"You look utterly pea green," exclaimed Lydia as she cantered past.

I hardly heard her: I was too terrified. There were about twenty riding school horses and ponies competing over a course of fifteen cross country jumps – brush fence, barrels, dry-stone wall, ditch, straw bales – nothing much more than two feet high but to me it looked like the Grand National course. I had walked round them hardly seeing them through my blur of fear.

Suddenly I thought I was going to faint.

"I can't do it," I said, hauling Bomber to a halt. "I can't. It doesn't matter what anyone says, I can't."

Angie marched up to me. She grasped Bomber's bit ring.

"Listen to me," she commanded. "This hat," and she held up David's bowler, "is a hat of courage. Wear it and you will see things as if you were David. They're tiny, easy-peasy jumps. Bomber's the best horse here. She could go round them blindfold. And you're the winner. THE WINNER. Put it on. See it all as David would see it."

I set the bowler firmly on my head. For a split second I was out of my stupid nervous self. I was David riding to win. The jumps were a challenge. Bomber's strength was on my side now. Not something to be afraid of. Together we would show them.

"You're next," said Angie, her flaming red curls frizzing round her face, her marine green eyes staring up at me. "You are going to win because you're wearing *the* hat."

At the sound of Miss Peel's whistle Bomber plunged forward. For a second I felt my usual fear choking me.

"The hat," screamed Angie. "You're wearing the hat. See it the way David would."

Although her words were torn away by our speed I heard them. "Ride at the jump," I told myself. "Ride at it."

I sank my weight down into my stirrups, balanced forward over Bomber's withers. I felt the table-top of her back lift over the first obstacle, a post and rails, and I was with her over the jump. Not left behind as I always was, but gloriously with her as she landed.

"It *is* the hat," I thought and was still laughing at the ridiculous notion of a hat helping me to jump when the brush jump was ahead of me; was beneath me; was behind me and we were galloping on to a ditch with low rails on either side.

"On you go Bomber!" I yelled for her speed was no longer anything to be afraid of. It was Bomber's courage that would make me, feeble, pathetic Kate Dawes into a winner. For the first time in my life I was really riding. I had left all my nervousness behind me. I was enjoying every second, wanting the galloping and the leaping to go on and on, never to stop.

Bomber cleared the last obstacle of straw bales in a surging plunge and we were through the finishing posts.

"You were clear," screamed Angie. "You were fantastic, brilliant, amazing."

"It was the hat!" I gasped breathlessly, throwing myself to the ground and making much of Bomber.

"Well!" exclaimed David, looking straight at me, no longer seeing me as Kate Dawes who was scared to jump, who was nothing but a coward.

"It was your hat," I told him, waving it at him. "When I was wearing it I could have jumped anything."

"And my horse," said David. "We were some partnership in the old days."

He held out his hand for his bowler and I gave it to him. Suddenly he burst out laughing. "This isn't my hat," he said.

"I got it from your hallstand," said Angie indignantly.

"And you'd better return it the second we get back. It's Dad's bowler. Never been further than the bank in its life. Kate would have known about it if she'd come off on her head wearing that."

"So you see," said Angie, never one not to make the most of a situation. "It wasn't the hat. It was you."

I didn't win. Lydia did. I wasn't even placed because somewhere I had missed out an obstacle. But it didn't matter, didn't matter a bit.

"I'll take Bomber on tomorrow's ride," I said to Angie as we stood at my gate discussing our day, and the thought was delight and brimming excitement, for I could ride now. I could jump.

"Well, don't forget your hat," said Angie.

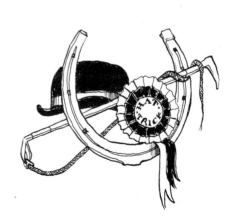

Careers with Ponies

Practically everyone who loves ponies thinks about a career with them at some time, but when they look into the long-term prospects, they often think again! Let there be no doubt about it, working with ponies is often hard, heavy and dirty, in all kinds of weather, for long hours, and for scant financial reward. This is why, out of every ten school-leavers who decide to work with horses or ponies, six will have fallen by the wayside within two years. Instead they opt for easier, better paid work, and limit their hours spent in equine company to weekends and holidays.

A career with ponies is not for the half-hearted, but those who do stay the course can find their work totally absorbing and satisfying; and for the really dedicated and well-trained there are both congenial and well-paid jobs.

Groom

The most obvious career with ponies is that of a groom. Training can never begin too early and as many riding schools actually need voluntary labour, enthusiasts who are still at school can get basic training in stable management in return for some hard work at weekends. This is an ideal way to find out if you are suited to life as a groom. A continual round of mucking out, feeding, grooming and exercising horses can be a monotonous grind to some, but others find real pleasure and satisfaction in a shining horse standing in a spotless stable, a clean yard, an orderly tackroom; even a neatly stacked muckheap!

After a period working as a full-time trainee in a well-run establishment, it will help your future prospects to gain some qualifications. Both the British Horse Society's Certificate of Horsemastership, and the Association of British Riding School's Groom's Diploma, require a knowledge of feeding, grooming, shoeing, saddlery and exercising as well as basic veterinary matters, grassland management, and the care of horses and ponies in transit. A driving licence will also be a bonus to any future employer.

Riding Instructor

If you think you have a sympathetic nature, can impart information clearly and simply, and are capable of inspiring others, then you might consider training as a riding instructor. You could teach at a children's riding school, or as a freelance, going out to help youngsters with their schooling at home. Teaching children and ponies requires a limitless supply of patience and tact – it takes a very special person to know when to be sympathetic and coax, and when to be firm and bully! Obviously, to be successful, you must be a competent rider yourself, as example is an essential teaching aid; so on top of the stable management skills you need as a groom – and until you become very highly qualified, a large part of your day will still be spent pushing a barrow – you will also require riding and teaching ability.

The British Horse Society Assistant Instructor's Certificate is a basic qualification for teachers. It is the first of a series of graduated examinations which are highly

A working pupil learns stable management as well as riding and teaching.

regarded throughout the world, and is divided into two parts. The first part is the Certificate of Horsemastership mentioned earlier, and the second the Preliminary Teaching Test. It shows that holders have achieved basic skills and are capable of instructing under supervision.

The usual way to train for a BHSAI Examination is to enrol at a BHS approved stables as a working pupil. This means that you work in return for your instruction; and the course, depending on the establishment and your own ability, can last from six months to two years. Living quarters are usually shared, and pupils often have to fend for themselves – cooking, washing and cleaning, all on top of a gruelling day in the stable yard! Not surprisingly the drop-out rate is 25%, and even then, very few people who pass the BHSAI go on to take the Intermediate Instructor's Examination which is the next rung in the ladder. If this sounds depressing, it isn't meant to be; most working pupils thrive in their spartan conditions and thoroughly enjoy their training once they have survived the culture shock!

Stud Assistant

Not everyone is keen either to ride or to teach and for them stud work might be the answer. As well as the usual stable routine, this involves the care of stallions and incoming mares for service, supervision of foaling and the handling of foals and youngstock. Even in the best run studs things sometimes go wrong – there may be complications in foaling, orphans which refuse to feed or surrogate mothers who refuse to adopt, so anyone intending to go in for stud work should be prepared to be a tower of strength in any emergency!

The National Pony Society's basic qualification is the Stud Assistant's Certificate which can be taken after a year's experience at the age of seventeen. The Diploma in Pony Mastership and Breeding is more advanced and candidates must be at least 21 years old with three year's experience.

The syllabus covers the production of native and riding ponies for the show ring which makes stud work a good starting point for anyone who eventually hopes to make a career with show ponies. Studs which breed the larger native and riding

The birth of a foal is a magical moment, but a routine job for a stud groom.

ponies often break and school their own youngstock and show mares and stallions under saddle, so there need be no lack of opportunity for those who enjoy riding.

Working with show ponies can be an arduous business, exercising and schooling, strapping, trimming and plaiting, with far more time spent travelling than anyone would ever imagine, and long, weary days away from home. It isn't all sparkling white rails, fluttering satin rosettes, and silver cups; mostly (and I say this from bitter experience), it's standing at the ringside in the driving rain, grinding your teeth because your prize exhibit is under the judge's eye with its ears back and its back humped against the rain like a dromedary, then getting stuck in a two-hour traffic jam on the way home! But there is nothing quite like the atmosphere of an English horse show, and on a good day, when the sun shines, and your pony stands at the top of the line, you will think that yours is the best and most rewarding job in the world.

Polo Groom

Someone with experience as a groom might consider working with polo ponies, although this is usually an occupation for the summer months only. Apart from the normal daily routine, a good deal of time is spent in the saddle, and riding a polo pony is an acquired skill. Because one hand needs to wield the polo stick the ponies are schooled to neck-rein, and refinements such as leg and seat aids are largely forgot-

123

ten. A good polo pony is very nippy indeed, capable of accelerating like a sports car and turning on a sixpence. Exercise takes place mainly at a canter on a large circle, changing rein and leg to keep the pony balanced and supple, and a polo groom may be seen exercising three ponies at once in this way! Exercise is somewhat monotonous, but practices and matches more than compensate for the hours spent circling in the paddocks. Polo grooms invariably become enthusiasts for the game as well as the champions of their ponies, and they enjoy the matches and the social life tremendously.

Polo jobs are not plentiful, but some are advertised in the horsy press at the beginning of the year. Applicants are likely to be more successful if they have experience and some knowledge of the game. A few Pony Clubs teach basic polo but, failing that, you should go to some matches armed with a library book on the subject.

These are just some of the careers you can find with ponies. As well as teaching, stud work, show ponies and polo, there are also seasonal openings at Holiday and Trekking Centres and opportunities to work as a groom in stables abroad. Whatever you want to do, make sure you stay at school long enough to fulfil the educational requirements of the job you want (the BHS for instance, demand 4 GCE 'O' levels for their A.I. examination). Then go out and get yourself a qualification to ensure that you are the one who gets one of those precious, congenial and well-paid jobs!

The address of the British Horse Society is:
The British Equestrian Centre,
Stoneleigh,
Kenilworth,
Warwickshire CV8 2LR.

Polo grooms rarely play, but get a ringside view of this exciting sport.